Win

Sin to

ABOUT THE AUTHOR

By the ripe old age of 20, Marc Lewis had flunked his A-levels, been turned down by every university and had been fired a dozen times. Not even Burger King would give him the pleasure of flipping burgers.

A remarkable eight years later and he's credited with winning the prestigious Guardian Scholarship to the School of Communication Arts, inventing Sir James Goldsmith's Referendum Party, launching the stand-up comedy movement in South Africa, revolutionising on-line advertising in the U.K. and building a $30 million business, Web Marketing.

After selling his company in 2001, Marc has been travelling the world, fast becoming one of the hottest consultants and speakers on the circuit, converting the masses into 'sinners'.

Marc lives in London with his partner, Rachel. His son, Luc, will never be a choir boy.

Marc Lewis is exclusively represented by:
SPEAKERS for BUSINESS
1-2 Pudding Lane,
London EC3R 8AB
United Kingdom
Tel: +44 (0)20 7929 5559
Fax: +44 (0)20 7929 5558
Email: marcl@which.net
www.sfb.co.uk

Win Sin to

Seven
deadly
steps to
success

Marc Lewis

CAPSTONE

First published 2002 by
Capstone Publishing Limited (A Wiley Company)
8 Newtec Place
Magdalen Road
Oxford OX4 1RE
United Kingdom
http://www.capstoneideas.com

CIP catalogue records for this book are available from the British Library and the US Library of Congress

ISBN 1-84112-311-0

Designed and typeset by Baseline, Oxford, UK
Printed and bound by T.J. International
This book is printed on acid-free paper

Substantial discounts on bulk quantities of Capstone books are available to corporations, professional
associations and other organisations.

Please contact Capstone for more details on +44 (0)1865 798 623 or (fax) +44 (0)1865 240 941 or (e-mail)
info@wiley-capstone.co.uk.

CONTENTS

For Rachel

ACKNOWLEDGEMENTS

Coming from a background in advertising agencies, dot-coms, publishing, consultancy and entertainment, it's fair to say I'm used to having my ego stroked. Writing is a lonely job by comparison, made easier with the help of countless friends and colleagues, many of whom I'll probably forget to thank until the day after the book goes into print.

Thanks first and foremost to my father, the most important teacher I've ever had. When he went bankrupt he demonstrated how to overcome adversity and taught me that there is no such thing as failure. When the house was taken away, he taught me that family is greater than material wealth. When I started out in business he taught me to make my own mistakes. When I became a millionaire he taught me to reach for the stars, but to keep my feet on the ground.

Thanks to my mother who continues to teach me to question everything, to keep my ears and eyes open and my head held high.

Thanks to my friends for putting up with my eccentricities, my highs and lows and my bad habits.

Thanks to my researchers, Ian, Mark and Chris for thousands of hours of trawling.

Thanks to my publishers for taking a chance, for their faith, support and counselling.

Thanks to my PR and to Lord Bell in particular, who has been an inspiration to me since the first day we met. It really is ironic that the most honest, straight-up businessman I've ever met comes from the world of advertising and politics.

Thanks to everyone at Speakers International for their advice, support, encouragement and enthusiasm. Harriet Beveridge, who worked like a trooper on the exercises in *Sin to Win*, tells me she has a lust to get her name in print. What kind of man would I be to turn down a woman's lust?

Thanks to the CEOs, MDs and Chairmen from all the companies I interviewed while writing this book. In particular, I would like to thank John Towers of MG Rover, Alan Hughes of First Direct, Michael Jackson of Channel 4 and Gordon Pell of Royal Bank of Scotland.

Finally, thanks to Rachel. You make me want to sin.

INTRODUCTION

There are more millionaires in England

than practising Catholics

FACT

THE BIBLE ISN'T JUST THE BEST SELLING personal development book of all time, it's the best selling book of all time. Hundreds of millions of people have had their attitudes altered and their mindsets shifted through the scriptures printed in 'The Good Book'.

We call them Christians.

But are they happy? Have they reached their full potential? Are they winners?

It's hardly surprising that the Bible can proudly boast the title of being a number one, worldwide best seller. Until 1477, the Church had a monopoly on printing. While Murdoch eliminates his competition either by buying or squeezing them out, the Church banned printing companies under the premise that they were owned and operated by the devil, a character from its own book. They protected their position at the top of the pile by sweeping away the competition – and burning them at the stake. Even Murdoch would find that a touch harsh.

No book tours were organised for the first edition of The Bible. There were no limited edition, signed copies. It wasn't necessary. The Church was the Government of the time. It made the rules, charged taxes, judged its people, decided who went to Heaven and who to Hell and then, in a fit of fair play, burned both categories at the stake. The Church, in short, ran our lives not merely with a rod of iron but with a whole arsenal of rods, which would rain down on a fearful populace like a nuclear defence system at the drop of a sinful hat.

As recompense for accepting the Bible, followers were forced to work either directly or indirectly for the Church. Peasants worked on the Church's farms and builders toiled, constructing ornate temples. Soldiers were sent on Church missions to find new lands for the Church to rule.

Christianity became the first global business.

What makes more sense?
To put your faith in something
that has never been proved or explained,
or to invest your faith in yourself?

At its peak, Christianity was the Microsoft of its day. Microsoft (as Lotus, Sun Microsystems and Sage will testify) covets its position in the marketplace. So too did Christianity. It needed to.

Philosophers were finding their voices, teaching the concept of free will. Alien to the teachings of Christianity, it was thought that we all controlled our own destinies – we could be anything we wanted to be. This was great news for the low-income earners, the majority of Christian followers, as they had scarcely any food on the dinner table, a short life expectancy and, let's face it, very little in the way of fun. The concept of free will, allowing the individual to improve their lot, had the potential to tempt peasants farming the land to down their tools in their droves. The Church was outraged and scared. Suddenly, it had competition.

The family of Christian churches, which, like real families, only ever gets together at Christmas and then with marked reluctance, were quick to identify its problem. Mankind's actions, it was concluded, are governed by one of three sets of laws: the law of God, the law of the land or the law of personal motives. The Church controlled the first two sets of laws, needing the third for a full house. The Seven Deadly Sins, a moral code designed with the sole intent of holding back our progress, were created. Not by God, but by mankind.

Pride, it was decided, was the most serious of the sins – probably because self-belief posed the greatest threat to the Church. It was feared that, as they learned free will, peasants would be envious of their taskmaster's position in society and want to improve their own status in life. So Envy was made a sin too. Gluttony was invented to combat unease caused by famine. Lust, the sin of craving for carnal pleasure, appears absurd and Victorian at first glance. But the Church couldn't risk its subjects deriving pleasure from anything other than the rule of God. Under the title Anger, it became a sin to be passionate enough about anything to want to change the status quo – such as religion. Avarice made it a sin to aspire to material goods, particularly those that belonged to the Church. Refusing to work for the Church, or follow any of the first six sins was considered slothful – the seventh of the sins.

Christianity had a new blockbuster on its hands. The sins were memorable and all-encompassing. Even those of us who have never been regular churchgoers remember more or less what they are. It was a moment of marketing genius by the Church. Seven is a clever number. It sounds good. It markets well. It is no coincidence that so many of Hollywood's most successful movies have included that number in their title, nor that so many brand names have employed it to such effect. Pub quizzes, the world over, are full of teams proudly reeling off the names of all of Snow White's seven dwarves or the actors who played each of the *Magnificent Seven*. There isn't an ageing, overweight club comedian who doesn't include a joke about "7 Up" or a "Party Seven" in his warm-up act, even though that latter brand hasn't been available for many years.

Islam. Judaism. Christianity. Buddhism.
They all think they're right.

What does that tell you?

Christianity continued to prosper until the onslaught of communication and education. With education comes knowledge, with knowledge comes power, and with power comes self-belief, the deadliest of the sins. Slowly, the Church found its grasp over society crumbling. It's not taboo not to be Christian any more – good news for other religions. In the seventeenth century it was illegal to be Jewish in England, for example. Sinners were burned alive.

While Christianity is no longer the power force it once was, the sins remain to this day. In a throw-back to medieval times, we're made to feel dirty for committing the sin of lust, conceited for possessing pride and miserly for employing the sin of avarice. The laws, invented to stifle free will, continue to suffocate us today.

My intention, in writing *Sin to Win*, isn't to question the existence of a god, nor the validity in following Christianity, or any other religion. The last thing I need is a Fatwah and, besides, I don't have the intelligence to argue for or against things I don't understand. Instead, my objective is to make clear how obeying each of the seven sins holds us back from reaching our full potential.

Perceptions of 'winning' will differ from person to person. We each have the right to measure our own value of success. Some might equate success to earning more money, driving a faster car or owning a larger house. Others may find their definition of success in a secure, loving family or through close friendships. Businesses might measure their success by size in the marketplace, profit or number of customers.

Whatever your personal goals are, committing to the seven deadly sins will give you the tools to realise them. The rest is up to you, and your free will.

All successful companies commit at least one
of the Seven Deadly Sins

FACT.

What does Rolls Royce stand for, if not pride? When Avis decided to beat Hertz and pledged to try harder to become the world's biggest car rental company, they displayed nothing less than naked envy. When Richard Branson enters into court actions against British Airways or Camelot, he fights for even greater personal and corporate success with anger. When Shell, BP and Esso preserve their margins by ignoring fuel protesters and hiding under governmental skirts they employ sloth with unrivalled skill. It was covetousness that spurred Ford to try to buy Ferrari and it was Fiat's corporate lust that beat them, forcing Ford to vent their envious desires on Aston Martin and Jaguar instead. And if Microsoft doesn't prove there's nothing wrong with a good strong dose of old-fashioned gluttony, nothing ever will.

Forget what you learned at Sunday school. Ignore what the English teacher taught. Dispense with every word all the other teachers beat into you. Wipe from your mind every lecture and symposium at college and university. If you take pride in your work, your home, your car, your yacht or simply your bank balance; if you are envious of others' success and crave even better for yourself; if you want more from your life, but prefer the easy route to achieving your goals, then you are committing each and every one of the Seven Deadly Sins.

All that remains is to learn how to commit them profitably.

Ignore the lessons contained in this book,
and you'll end up paying Sin Tax at the highest rate.

FACT.

PRIDE

is excessive belief in one's own abilities, that interferes with the individual's recognition of the grace of God. It has been called the sin from which all others arise.
Pride is also known as Vanity.

ENVY

is the desire for others' traits, status, abilities, or situation.

GLUTTONY

is an inordinate desire to consume more than that which one requires.

LUST

is an inordinate craving for immediate self-gratification.

ANGER

is manifested in the individual who spurns forgiveness and opts instead for revenge.
It is also known as Wrath.

AVARICE

is the desire for material wealth or gain, ignoring the realm of the spiritual.
It is also called Greed.

SLOTH

is the avoidance of physical or spiritual work.

♦ Sin to WIN

H AVE YOU EVER SEEN A FLY trying to get through a closed window? It smacks itself against the glass again and again. It's never going to get through, but it just keeps trying the same tactic again and again.

If you do what you've always done, you'll get what you've always got. Same tactics means same results. Presumably, you are reading this book because you want different results, which means doing things differently, thinking differently and acting differently.

Seven chapters lie ahead of you. Each chapter focuses on one of the Seven Deadly Sins, explaining why you should commit to becoming a Sinner. The revelations after each chapter will give you the tools to do so.

These revelations are about putting your money where your mouth is and trying some different approaches. Some of them may seem a little weird to begin with. Treat them with the same respect you paid to your first pint of beer – strange, exciting and an acquired taste at first, but well worth the effort.

The Sin of

PRIDE

'I have nothing to declare but my genius.'

Oscar Wilde

*'I have nothing to declare but 200 Rothmans
and a litre bottle of Smirnoff.'*

George Best

P RIDE IS FIRMLY AT THE NUMBER ONE SLOT on the list of Deadly Sins, and yet is far from being an obvious trait to be deplored. If your kids do well at school, you will quite rightly be proud of them. If you work hard, you are to be congratulated in taking pride in a job well done. If you dress well, you are praised for taking pride in your appearance. If you are included in the Queen's birthday honours list in recognition of your life-long services to charities for distressed donkeys, you will quite rightly feel proud to be photographed outside Buckingham Palace displaying your shiny gong to the press. Your pride won't even be lessened by the certain knowledge you will be pictured on page seventeen of the *Daily Telegraph* dressed in a suit and hat that would have been considered unfashionably passé by David Lloyd George. What exactly, then, does the Church believe is wrong with a sense of pride? It is true to say that pride can be misplaced? When Sooty mentor Harry Corbett was awarded his OBE for a career of selfless devotion to glove puppetry, even he was a proud man. His pride wasn't remotely dented by the fact that he had been honoured thanks only to a simple typing error, and that his medal had actually been intended for the fine actor, Harry H. Corbett. No harm at all was done to Harry Corbett's social standing, nor the fees he received for future bookings.

You want to be successful. Set out your aims.
Make a good long list in order of priority.
Now throw it away.
It is your achievements you must set out.

The difference between a loser and a winner is that between aim and achievement.

This isn't the sort of pride that the Bible has such great concern to eliminate. How could it? The fourth-century Greek monks who wrote much of the original biblical text might have had supreme insight into the workings of our Lord and in heaven, and Beelzebub in his burning satanic hell hole, but they could hardly be expected to guess that 1500 years later a future queen of England would be pinning a medal on Sooty's furry little chest.

Pride can be interpreted in a variety of different ways. Like as not, if your alcohol-ravaged, uninsured teenage son crashes the family car and supplies the excuse that he was distracted by the news that his fifteen-year-old girlfriend was carrying their child, you will say 'I hope you're proud of yourself'. Little wonder, then, that we grow up confused about the Sin of Pride. In a day-to-day sense, the word 'pride' is used simply to express an understandable recognition of one's own worth.

S A I N T   O R   S I N N E R ?

Joshua Norton, born in London in 1819, declared himself Emperor of the United States in 1859 by sending notification to the *San Francisco Bulletin*. He issued his own banknotes, sent orders to official bodies and made tours of the city streets. When he was arrested on the grounds of being a lunatic, public uproar forced his release and from then on the police saluted him. He demanded that a bridge be built between San Francisco and Oakland and when, 50 years later, the Golden Gate Bridge was constructed it was dedicated to him. In 1880 his funeral was attended by 20,000 mourners.

There are fine dividing lines between self-pride and conceit, between conceit and arrogance and between arrogance and an ego the size of Devon.

However, there are fine dividing lines between self-pride and conceit, between conceit and arrogance and between arrogance and an ego the size of Devon. An all-consuming belief in one's own worth is seen as excluding any appreciation of the worth of others. In many fields this can even be the source of adulation. Truly great sportsmen and women don't win by applauding the great skills of their opponents, but equally, they won't win if they fail to recognise them. When John McEnroe was throwing his broken racquet round the Wimbledon Centre Court, claiming every point was his, and hurling abuse at everyone who would listen and even more who wouldn't, it was an expression of his own therapy to overcome the certain knowledge that Bjorn Borg was, at that stage, better than him.

That wasn't important to McEnroe's longer-term career. Any tennis fan will quote the 1981 men's singles final as one of the finest displays ever by two sportsmen, and most will explain how McEnroe fought back to save the fourth set and match. He did fight back to take the set, but he didn't win the match. Even so, we all think he did. His therapy certainly worked on us. He thought of himself as a winner, we began to think of him as a winner, and in later years, he became a winner. But the perception came first. McEnroe skilfully employed the Sin of Pride.

Look around at the all the highly successful people you know.
Do they actually look successful?
Of course they do.
How would you know they're successful otherwise?

The appearance of achievement leads to achievement.

However, if the striker for Maidstone Town FC looks forward to a second round FA cup tie having convinced himself and his team that they can beat Manchester United hollow at Trafford Park, because MU are about as threatening as a coach party of nuns at a Cliff Richard concert, he is in for shock. There will be no future trip to Wembley followed by a run around the pitch waving a large piece of silverware for his team. In fact, of course no team will be going anywhere near Wembley Stadium in the foreseeable future, since the government's team of crack planners who negotiated its re-design brief are themselves less threatening than a coach party of nuns at a Cliff Richard concert. They do not commit the Sin of Pride.

Pride is the first and most important sin not because it is the most heinous. Far from it. Pride is in fact that tricky little blighter that isn't always even a bad thing. This confusion arises from the tendency of words in the English language to change their meaning over time. Until the beginning of the nineteenth century, if someone were described as being 'sophisticated' this meant that they were pretending to be what we now describe as sophisticated.

With the growth in global communication, and English as the lingua franca of popular music, the Internet and satellite television, this process continues on apace. Thanks to pop culture, 'bad' suddenly means what we used to call 'good', 'wicked' means what we used to call 'very good', and 'posh' means someone we used to call 'sophisticated' up until the beginning of the nineteenth century. Even a simple little word like 'posh' has changed its meaning overnight, thanks to a very successful and rich young woman, who is as posh as prawn cocktail washed down with warm Liebfraumilch.

Victoria Beckham may not be the most talented singer in the world, in fact at most of her concerts she probably isn't the most talented singer in the room, but ...

Victoria Beckham may not be the most talented singer in the world, in fact at most of her concerts she probably isn't the most talented singer in the room, but the Sin of Pride goes a long way to solving the minor pop music drawback of not being able to sing a note unless accompanied by a tape recorder. She and her fellow Spice Girl conspirators were amongst the highest earning pop music acts ever, eclipsing the likes of the Beatles, the Rolling Stones and Elvis Presley. In short, the Spice Girls are a seriously successful business.

'Pride' is one of those words that has acquired a new meaning, while still retaining the original in parallel. The word 'quite' is similar. If your wife's new dress were

SAINT OR SINNER?

'There are many dying children out there whose last wish is to meet me.'

Could it be Santa Claus, the most successful postman in the world, who uttered these immortal words? Or the Pope perhaps? No, it was none other than Mr Baywatch himself, David Hasselhof. Listed in the *Guinness Book of Records* as the world's 'Most Watched TV Star' thanks to the massive global popularity of *Baywatch* and *Knight Rider*, Hasselhof is also a multi-platinum-selling recording artist who has had number one singles in Germany. Scary.

described as 'quite nice', she might not be over impressed. But if it was considered to be 'quite delightful', then 'quite' has changed from meaning 'sort of' to 'completely'. Where is this short history of modern English usage leading us? It is leading us towards understanding not only exactly what we mean, but also exactly what is understood by what we intend to mean. Meaning is both given and taken, both implied and inferred. To most readers of this book, the written word 'pain' indicates that sensation felt at the dentist when he presents his £2000 bill for some bridge work that took all of twenty minutes to complete. To a French speaker, it means a crusty loaf so long and spindly that it can't be put in a carrier bag without being bent in half. His actual inference is a world away from our intended implication. Ones man's pride is another man's perceived arrogance.

Do you always make sure the signals you make are understood
as you intended?

Pride is the appearance of achievement.

Superbia sounds like the invention of an estate agent who needs a new euphemism to
describe an unfashionable part of the outer city, which he thinks should be on the up.
It is in fact another biblical term for the Sin of Pride. It comes from Latin, and means
literally 'aiming at what is above'. The Roman Empire was built on superbia, that hunger
for what is bigger and better and it is very possibly the Roman model that led to its
inclusion as the primary sin. Having conquered most of Europe, large tracts of the
Middle East and much of North Africa, the Roman mood passed from pride in the sense
of a passion for self-improvement, to a sense of power-induced intoxication and, if the
history books are to be believed, an intoxication-induced sense of self-satisfied euphoria.

The Roman Empire reigned supreme for seven centuries and then, within a matter of a few short decades, imploded under the force of its own vacuous self-regard.

The Roman Empire reigned supreme for seven centuries and then, within a matter of
a few short decades, imploded under the force of its own vacuous self-regard. In its
day, the very term 'Roman' became a byword for excellence. A Roman road was a well-
mettaled arrow-straight thoroughfare users of the M6 can only dream about. Roman
baths meant the finest heating and hydraulics engineering the world had ever seen
and would not see again for another 1000 years. Roman law represented the fairest
judicial system a criminal could hope to face, and yet the Roman Empire collapsed.

Today, we have a similar term to represent the pinnacle of excellence, and it is no
coincidence that the name comes from the motor industry, one that would be an

emaciated shadow of the giant we see today were it not for pride. To be hailed as providing the 'Rolls-Royce' of any service or product is be the recipient of the highest accolade any marketing manager could wish for.

Just like that of the Romans', the Rolls Royce Empire was founded purely on pride. Lots of us need cars, but no one needs a Rolls Royce. Precious few of us will ever even ride in one, let alone own any of their models and yet for very nearly the whole of the twentieth century, from the day a gifted engineer and an aristocrat looking for something to do with his inheritance wheeled their first model out of a Derby garage, you could ask anyone in the world who knew what a

THE SIN OF PRIDE – NIKE

Nike is an *über*-brand. A phonetic translitteration of the ancient Greek word for victory, it has built its success on fusing its own self-belief with the self-belief and aspiration of its consumers. Just do it.

The company started out making trainers, stomping on all comers, before extending its reach into every corner of the sporting industry.

Its omnipresent swoosh now bedecks the caps, chest, and feet of the world's leading athletes and sportsmen. Everything about the brand, from its progressive and cutting edge design to its imaginative use of instantly recognisable sporting figures in advertising, oozes self-belief.

And nothing symbolizes this self-belief more effectively than its huge flagship stores in some of the world's glamour capitals. Huge department stores, that appear almost as museums, glorify the name of Nike and elevate it well above mere sporting brand.

motor car was who they thought made the best in the world, and they would say 'Rolls Royce'.

Fine cars, they undoubtedly are, but like all prestige and performance road vehicles they have nothing to do with being the practical solution of how to get yourself and the family from A to B. There isn't a motorist in the world who needs a 180 mph Ferrari or a six-speed Aston Martin or an Alfa Romeo with Formula One style gear paddles mounted on the steering wheel. True, some owners will argue that they use their machines at weekend for sporting purposes, going racing or taking in track days, but they could just as easily buy a purpose built track car for a small fraction of the price and use a second-hand Ford during the week. Pride is the motivation that has most of us clamouring for a new car with all the right bells and whistles every few years, not transport needs. Rolls Royce is a classic case of exploiting pride to its fullest.

There was even a manufacturer of extruded plastic receptacles who proudly boasted that his product was the Rolls Royce of dustbins.

Rolls Royce Motors (they are no longer connected with the aero-engine arm) not unnaturally go to extreme lengths jealously to guard the use of their good name. Every conceivable type of product has at one time or another been described as 'the Rolls Royce of' whatever. Over-keen domestic appliance manufacturers have advertised the Rolls Royce of washing machines and the Rolls Royce of vacuum cleaners. There have been the Rolls Royces of watches, bicycles, typewriters. . . you name it, there has been a Rolls Royce of it. There was even a manufacturer of extruded plastic receptacles who proudly boasted that his product was the Rolls Royce of dustbins.

In fact, only one company has ever been officially sanctioned by the factory to borrow the name for advertising purposes, and that was the manufacturer of the Brough Superior Motorcycle, which was retailed during the 1920s and 1930s.

Mention the Brough Superior to any vintage motorcycle enthusiast and he will tell you two things about it: one, it was the Rolls Royce of motorbikes and two, it was a Brough Superior that killed T.E. Lawrence, the great British hero who rallied Arab tribesmen to fight on the allied side against the Turks during the First World War.

Lawrence of Arabia survived the most blood-thirsty four years of human massacre in the history of the world, only to die when he was thrown over the handle bars of

THE SIN OF PRIDE – OAKLEY

Oakley is a model of self-belief. Not only does the company sell a brand of idiosyncratic self-confidence in the form of its distinctive bow-shaped sunglasses, but its entire working culture reflects that same pride. It was set up back in 1975 with a determination to be youth-driven and original and has maintained that emphasis despite growing rapidly ever since. They work the way their customers live.

Just look at the way it describes itself – a technology company 'fueled by a raging distaste for mediocrity and a fierce devotion to innovation'. It talks about defying convention, reinventing concepts and its own mad science. It has fought to preserve this identity. The result – a global brand represented in more than 70 countries.

And the company makes the same demands of its customers. 'Being an Oakley consumer requires a willingness to think differently,' it said in a recent public letter. Disgruntled that its major retailer, Sunglass Hut, scaled back the number of Oakley items it will carry, the company told its customers to go out and find somewhere else to buy its products.

Now that takes some self-belief.

a Brough Superior just a few yards from his home on a Hampshire country lane. The irony was not wasted on the Brough Company, who went bust some years later, not because of the unfortunate demise of Lawrence, but rather because they really were making the Rolls Royce of motorcycles. And how many of us want to pay for that kind of quality engineering only to have to sit astride two wheels exposed to the freezing elements? No one really needs a Rolls Royce, and equally, no one really needs hypothermia.

Pride is certainly good, but it has its place. So well regarded is the very name 'Rolls Royce' that when, in 1971, it took its turn to collapse along the lines of the Roman Empire with debts of £200 million, the UK government was only too eager to bail it out. Such was the belief – in many respects blind belief – in the quality of its product that recovery was swift. The Rolls Royce reputation is founded entirely on pride.

The factory has never followed the traditional route to sales success. They rarely advertise. They have never entered into any kind of racing, while even the motorised shopping trolley manufacturer, Rover, sends cars to the Le Mans 24 Hour race. Rich foreigners queued by the thousand through the 1970s and 1980s to put their names down for the same car that the Queen of England rides in. Except that she doesn't. British heads of state have been driven in nothing but Daimlers ever since the motor car was invented. That is what Rolls Royce means to its proud owner: pride will overcome the tiresome reality of true fact.

Not only was Rolls Royce built on pride; it was also saved by it. Saved by the pride of an entire nation, 99.9% of whom had never even touched a Rolls Royce – not even to scrape a jealous set of house keys across its hand-finished paintwork.

Lawrence of Arabia survived the most blood-thirsty four years of human massacre in the history of the world, only to die when he was thrown over the handle bars of a Brough Superior just a few yards from his home...

So blinded are buyers by the brand that Volkswagen, one of the world's truly great success stories as manufacturers of affordable reliable transport and later inventors of the 'hot hatch' GTI concept that was needed by no-one but bought by millions, acquired Rolls Royce in 1998. Even VW felt that it could improve with a car like the Rolls Royce in its stable. The predictable squeals of anguish amongst traditional British admirers of the marque were loud enough to be heard in Berlin. Nor did it go unnoticed by the disgusted retired colonels of Tunbridge Wells that VW had manufactured aircraft components for German Messerschmidt and Fokker Wulf fighter planes during the Second World War, and that these had fought the Battle of Britain in the skies over London against British Spitfires and Hurricanes powered by Rolls Royce Merlin engines. So blinded were VW by the shining beacon of excellence that is the Rolls Royce name, that they failed to notice that one particular item was not included in the sale. They had acquired the factory, the designs, the work-force and the entire marketing and distribution infrastructure.

What they hadn't acquired was the name 'Rolls Royce' – the only thing they really needed. VW now make some very nice German Bentleys. Rolls Royce were free to sell the name elsewhere. Pride hadn't allowed them to even think of their own name in the same category as mere capital assets like a factory, assembly line or workforce.

Do you truly believe you are talented at your job?
Yes? Well stop it. It's ability you need, not talent.

Talent does not equal ability.

THE SIN OF PRIDE — DIRECT LINE

Direct Line is an excellent example of a company that has succeeded through corporate self-belief. Peter Woods, the company's founder, was totally convinced the world needed a new type of insurance company when he started out in Croydon, back in 1984.

Today, with over 3 million customers, Direct Line is the largest private motor insurer in the UK. It sells a new policy every six seconds and filters 15 million calls a year.

Typical for a Croydoner (and I should know, because I was one) Direct Line is always up for a fight, believing it has the brawn and the brain to take on anyone. In its short life-time, the company has developed a reputation for causing waves and challenging authority in various markets — unsurprisingly, to its financial benefit.

With stunts more commonly associated with Branson's Virgin empire than the staid insurance sector, Direct Line has assumed the role of 'public protector'. It took on established motor insurance companies and won. It lobbied the Office of Fair Trading over the unfair practice of banks and building societies, complaining that they were ripping off the great British public by restricting choice for home insurance, and won. They knew they were right. They had self-belief.

That abundant self-belief is no accident, it runs through the veins of Direct Line. As Myles Russel, a Board Director of the company explains:

'We're proud of creating a brand that, in a fairly short timescale, has become a super brand — a brand with 96% awareness. It's a brand that is associated with completely revolutionising the insurance industry. That's important to the staff, in terms of having pride in the organisation they work for.

I think to be proud of something you've achieved couldn't possibly be considered to be arrogant or conceited in any way. I think it's good for the company and for the employees — everybody from the top down — to feel they work for a company that's actually going places and that has actually got some success to it's credit.'

Another motor manufacturer who had supreme self-belief, but who happened to operate at the exact opposite end of the market spectrum, was Henry Ford. Henry Ford was a great one for the throw away one-liner. Every reader is now thinking of two short sentences:

One 'Any colour, so long as it's black.'
Two 'History is bunk.'

Henry Ford said neither. He said, 'Exercise is bunk. If you are healthy, you don't need it; if you are sick, you shouldn't take it.' That's pride. What he did say of history is that it is 'more or less bunk. It is tradition. We don't want tradition. We want to live in the present.' As for the colour of his 'only available in black' Model T, that was a music hall-style joke at the expense of cheap cars, in much the same way jokes were made later made about Skodas and Ladas. Worse than that, it was quite common in Britain between the wars to see garages displaying large signs that read 'No Fords'. That at one time 80% of all the cars in the world were Ford Model Ts, was neatly ignored by Ford's detractors, lovers of quality machines such as those made by Rolls Royce, Daimler, Lagonda, Riley, Wolsley and MG. Ford however, unlike that list of quality motor manufacturers, has never gone bust nor been taken over by a rival.

Being born talented is a waste of effort.
If your grass needs cutting, get a gardener.
If you need talent, buy some.

Talent is an optional luxury.

Even though Henry Ford didn't originate most of the quotations attributed to him, he was happy to let the world think he did. So where did Ford make a real mark? His true genius, surely, lay in inventing the mass assembly-line system of production. Except that he didn't. Mass production, through assembly of standard components, was devised by Eli Whitney as long ago as 1798. What Ford did was to apply this system on a constantly moving conveyer belt system, a system he copied from the one introduced in Liverpool in 1868 to shift bulk food goods.

Between 1908 and 1923, thanks to the massive sales of his Model T, a car which was almost undriveable even by the primitive standards of the day, Henry Ford amassed a personal fortune estimated at the equivalent value today of $14 billion. Not content with that tidy sum, Ford wanted to be even more successful and decided to build the V8 engine.

Again, the V8 was no original concept. It had been used before in up-market machines, but the lengthy manufacturing process necessary to produce two banks of four cylinders each in parallel was wholly unsuited to his cheap and cheerful mass production ethic. So he simply told his engineers to make a V8 in a single casting, just like they did with the old basic engines used in the Model T. His entire engineering department said that it couldn't be done. In short, the single cast V8 was impossible. Henry Ford was no talented engineer, so he didn't care about engineering impossibilities. He had supreme faith in his own ideas, so he simply told his engineers to get on with it and not to come back until they had fulfilled his command.

It took time, but the more time the engineers took, the more they realised that Ford had meant what he said and they risked imminent unemployment if they failed. Ford also knew that if his finest engineers had just spent a year or so failing to develop the impossible V8, they were unlikely to gain employment with a competitor. Eventually, they did discover a production method that worked, and the Ford V8 put Henry so far ahead of the competition that it took them 40 years to catch up.

When, in the 1990s, the modern Ford Corporation decided that they needed something a bit more up-market in the range, something that said 'special', they went out and bought Aston Martin and Jaguar. And when they started introducing new models with these brands, what was underneath? The sort of production methods forced upon the engineers by Henry Ford way back when. Lift up the bonnet of the latest supercharged Aston Martin and you'll find an engine that first found a home in a Ford Scorpio. Peel away the skin of the new X-Type Jaguar and you'll find a Mondeo engine, gearbox, front suspension, braking system, back axle and floorpan. Look at the windscreen and you'll find a Jaguar price sticker.

SAINT OR SINNER?

The fat-tongued master of mockney and the UK's television chef-du-jour, Jamie Oliver, has a pretty high opinion of himself. In a recent interview he told the the *Daily Telegraph*, 'At the moment I am the ambassador of British cooking across the world. I have done more for English food throughout the world in the past two years than anyone else has done in the past 100 years. I have put it on the map, for Crissakes.' Which is pretty cocky in anybody's book. But it hasn't stopped the 26-year-old amassing a fortune from his two television series, two best-selling books and series of Sainsbury's ads.

Leaders like Henry Ford have an unswerving belief in their own abilities, ideas and objectives, even if not one of them is original. They know there's a difference between merely jumping on a bandwagon, and taking over the controls of that bandwagon. They have pride by the skip load. Ford didn't have particularly marked abilities in any area except for his ability to believe in his ability. He gave us a handful of great one-liners he never actually said. He didn't invent the production line, but he made it a success, when no other motor manufacturer had even thought of the concept. And he copied, improved and cheapened the exclusive V8 engine and made it available to the masses and in so doing made his company future secure for the rest of the century and beyond.

Stephen Hawking can neither speak nor use any of his limbs.
He wrote one of the best-selling books of all time.
Neither you nor any of your friends have read beyond page eight.

Let pride give you ability.

Pride, in part, is a measure of inner happiness. It is about self-respect and the freedom to become elated over achievements. Boast when you get that big sale. Let everyone know that you are the best. Tell your boss, your co-workers and your customers that you are the tops, the bee's knees, the dog's dangly bits.

When, in the mid-1980s, British Airways felt they had an image problem, they put video booths in their major airport terminals and invited arrivals customers to tell them on tape how they felt about the service they had just received. Not surprisingly, few of them poured out unalloyed adulation. When Robert Louis Stevenson said, 'it is better to travel hopefully than to arrive' he obviously hadn't just spent fourteen hours in economy class with his knees around his ears, trying to eat a rubber chicken with a plastic fork.

So what did British Airways do with this catalogue of complaints from their fare-paying public? Did they go away and work on improving their service, chucking out seats to provide more leg-room and employing cordon bleu chefs on every flight? No they did not. That would be too much like expensive hard work. Instead, they simply told everyone that they were the 'World's Favourite Airline'. Lord King knew a bit about arrogance.

When challenged on this claim, as they frequently were, BA's executives proudly pointed to their passenger mile statistics, which were the highest in the world. If they carry more people over more miles than any other carrier, ergo they are the world's favourite. There is one minor flaw in their argument. They didn't carry more passengers further than anyone else. They came second in that league, to Aeroflot. As anyone who ever had the misfortune to have to fly with the old Soviet carrier, its Tupolevs so laden down with emergency fuel and military hardware that there was no room for luxuries such as food or drink, will testify, it would take a leap of imagination of Olympic Gold Medal winning standard to describe them as the world's favourite airline.

But, by British Airways' measure, that is what Aeroflot was. 'However', pointed out BA's keen young marketing team, 'Aeroflot only carries that number of passengers because they've been given all their routes by the government.' Fair point. But where did British Airways get its routes? From the government, who handed them on a plate to the newly invigorated flag carrier at privatisation. Whether Lord King actually believed that BA actually ever was or ever will be the world's favourite airline is not only debatable, but also wholly irrelevant. Such a subjective judgement is almost impossible to measure. If the travelling public see advertising stating this as fact, and advertising in Britain is required by law to be legal, decent and honest, then, by some measure or other, it must be true. It did in fact become true, because Lord King said so. It was his airline and he knew best. The expression 'The World's Favourite Airline' is now inextricably linked in our minds with British Airways.

These people and organisations share one common trait. Thanks to their predilection to commit the Sin of Pride, they instinctively know the difference between management and leadership and they have an unswerving faith in their own leadership qualities. So overpowering is this faith that people like Ford probably never even thought about it.

But you are not a Henry Ford; at least not yet. So stop and think about the way you function. You are probably reasonably successful in your own field.

Do you do things right?
Almost certainly, but that is successful management.

Successful leadership is doing the right things.

Only you can decide for yourself what the right things are, but that's a skill that can be learned to the point it becomes an instinct. For example, imagine yourself in the position of the sales executive who once worked in premises that had previously been occupied by a completely unrelated business. The office retained the telephone number, which went with the building. (This was in the days before BT privatisation, when it was considered a faster option to move your business to a new telephone than to have a new line or number installed in existing premises.)

Unsurprisingly, many calls were received which were intended for the previous tenant, and a keen and otherwise efficient young assistant would routinely answer these telephone queries with the question 'Who do you think you are talking to?' In his mind, this was a perfectly reasonable response to a request for details of a product that clearly wasn't in their range. But to the callers, this can only have sounded like totally unwarranted arrogance. Many chose immediately to take their business elsewhere.

What would you do? Should you explain to the assistant that his telephone attitude was being misunderstood and that he should politely explain that the company the caller was trying to reach had moved and possibly even that his was a completely different company, selling completely different products? You might think so.

What he actually did was to instruct the assistant to take any order placed, regardless of what it was actually for. He replaced unwarranted arrogance with warranted arrogance. He ignored the protests of the assistant, who was used only to accepting orders for products on his list, and then added these new items to the product range. He got them at trade price from the previous tenants, who had for some reason left their new number pinned on the wall of the sales office. Anything new that couldn't be supplied wouldn't be a problem, as the failure to deliver would be blamed on the other company. This sales executive was a committed pride sinner all right. Even more so when a satisfied new customer said how happy he was to have changed supplier, as he'd been so incensed by the attitude of his old one that he'd slammed the phone down on them just a few days before.

The Ten Commandments
of committing the sin of

PRIDE

---

1 If you are the best, then take pride in saying you are.

It's no use having this knowledge and keeping it to yourself. But you don't have to run about simply saying 'I'm the best'. Act as if the fact is a given. Follow the example of the Indianapolis 500 driver who used to arrive late at pre-race briefings every year and wander in nonchalantly and say 'Hi guys, what you doin'? Trying to figure out who's gonna come in second?'. Make your superiority an assumption, not an announcement.

2 If you aren't the best, then take pride in saying say you are.

There is no such thing as a mind reader. It doesn't matter what you think you know, it only matters what you appear to know. You are the only one who can decide what is in your head. You are the only one who can let other people think what is inside your head. And what they think is in your head, is automatically in their heads. If you don't appear to know within yourself that you are the best, you won't be.

3 There is no such thing as a proud loser.

From now on, your motto is: 'Show me a good loser, and I'll show you a loser.'

Make it known there'll be problems if you don't get your own way. When Henry Ford ignored his staff who thought he made impossible demands, they knew there'd be trouble if they didn't prove themselves wrong. When Lord King said his airline was to be known as the world's favourite, he stopped listening until it was. John McEnroe never lost. He was only ever unfairly robbed of his victory.

4 Show the world you are proud of your success.

Let it be known which expensive car you drive and how big your house is. Name-drop without shame. If there's anybody remotely within earshot, Sir David Frost always greets his mobile phone callers very loudly:

'Boutros Boutros! So looking forward to seeing you again. By the way – Bill and Hillary asked me to send their love'. What a surprise that is to his plumber on the other end of the line.

And if anyone wants to know exactly where you find the space to land your new helicopter anywhere near your Monte Carlo apartment, it's on your yacht – of course.

5 Be proud of your success, even if you haven't had any yet.

If you can afford only to stay at a cheap hotel, arrange to meet your client in the foyer of the expensive one across town. Get there early, go up to the first floor landing where you can observe the entrance. As your potential customer arrives, bound down the stairs to greet him, doing up your tie and apologising for being so busy. After the meeting, tell reception you don't want to be disturbed that afternoon and ask them to take messages. As even the top end of the hotel trade pays only the minimum wage, a crisp tenner should do the job. When the client tries to call you there, you'll be able to pick up your deal-clinching calls later. If you have nothing else to do, wait near reception and take the call with a cheery 'I was just passing by on my way out to the bank. You know what Coutts are like when it comes to signing paperwork.'

6 Be proud to know best.

Only use facts that suit your story. If the appropriate facts don't suit your story, choose facts that do. If there aren't any, make them up. Use spurious statistics. To quote Vic Reeves, '78.5% of statistics are made up on the spur of the moment.' If you want to prove beyond mathematical doubt that your sales are growing by over 20% per year when they are as flat as a billiard table, evidence will be found in the last six month's figures available when growth was over 10%, which will be August over February, guaranteed. August, with 31 days, is 10.7% longer than February with 28.

If it suits, you can prove anything, no matter how implausible. Official UK government statistics prove that drunken drivers are safer than sober ones. According to their reports, drunken drivers cause 35% of car crashes. Take all the sober ones off the road and improve road safety by 65% at a stroke. Your knowledge is strength. Your knowledge is entirely yours.

7 Be proud to know everything.

Knowing everything everyone wants to hear sells. This is all the more impressive and unarguable if it happens to be your personal opinion of a matter totally unrelated to the business at hand. Over small talk, impress that Executive Vice-President of Purchasing that you could only recommend one exclusive private school for his kids now he's moved here from Houston, but make it the one he's already chosen for them. You know which it is because that morning you rang his secretary, explaining that you met her boss at a golf day a few weeks back when he recommended a good school, and would she kindly remind you which one it was?

She'll know. She wrote all the letters of application and sent out the cheques. Telling the VP that he's made the only good choice, without prompting, makes him tell himself that you are the only good choice.

8 Pride replaces formal qualifications.

You are proud enough not to need them. Think of the story about the heart surgeon who gets up in the morning to find he has a blocked toilet. It won't flush, and he is in danger of flooding his expensively appointed bathroom with solid matter wrapped in Andrex's finest. So, he calls a plumber who arrives carrying a stick with a rubber plunger on the end and clears the mess in about three minutes.

'That'll be seventy-five quid', he says.
'Seventy-five pounds for three minutes work?' says the incredulous heart surgeon, 'That's more than I make!'

'I know', says the plumber, 'I didn't make this kind of money when I was a heart surgeon'.

Croydon Council recently advertised for a trainee gardener to help tend their municipal gardens. The last line of the ad read: 'Age range 21-25. Would suit graduate.' How many proud MSc's would apply for that little number?

9 Pride allows you to say 'yes'.

Never admit that you can't do something. If a customer comes into your carpet shop carrying a greasy black plastic box-shaped item and asks 'Do you test car batteries?', then say you do. You automatically know something about the customer. He is new to the area, otherwise why does he think your shop is the place to go for car battery service? If he's just moved into the area, he needs stuff for his new house – carpets, for example. While your assistant is out the back of the shop testing the battery, sell the newcomer his new carpets and quietly remember to add an extra fifty quid to the bill. This will cover the cost of the new battery your assistant is out buying from Halfords, to magically reappear as the customer's refurbished item. You really can do anything. You only have to say you can. Don't even think about the things you can't do – they no longer exist. 'Can't do' is in the past.

10 Let Pride enable you.

Pride is power. Power corrupts. Absolute power corrupts absolutely.

Power enables. Absolute power enables absolutely. Absolute pride enables absolutely.

Exercise on

PRIDE

Imagine your state of mind on a scale of one to ten. When you are at one, you feel lousy. Everything goes wrong. The traffic is awful; you are late for work and get a blasting from your boss. You spill coffee over yourself before going to see a client, they cancel the contract and your quarterly figures are shot to pieces. In short, life is a series of knock backs in which the only excitement is the prospect of retiring one day with a carriage clock. If you're lucky.

When you are at a ten you are cock-a-hoop, unstoppable, everything you touch turns to gold. You know you are a god. You clinch a million pound deal and go to the pub to celebrate. You see Kylie Minogue at the bar, chat her up and she begs you for a hot date. You are on a roll.

Why are some days great and others lousy? Well, most people see the world like this:

RESULTS ⟶ BEHAVIOUR ⟶ STATE

They believe that the results we get dictate our behaviour, which in turn conditions our state – how we feel. 'I had a bad day – what do you expect after the traffic in the morning', it is a downward spiral. You become a victim of events.

The key to the Sin of Pride is to see the world like this:

STATE ⟶ BEHAVIOUR ⟶ RESULTS

Then it is an upward spiral. Feeling proud means you are much more likely to get results. Getting results increases your pride.

And the 'good news' is that we can control our state. You can literally conjure up a feeling of pride out of thin air in a couple of minutes. Here are a couple of ways to:

Feel good for no good reason.

Sit the way you would sit if you were feeling bored, miserable, depressed. Notice how you are sitting.

Now sit the way you would sit if you were feeling immensely proud, chuffed to bits, knowing you are a total god. Again, notice how you are sitting and notice how you feel.

Why did you move? I didn't ask you to move, but I'd bet my trousers that you did. Why? Because our physiology – that's the way we use our body – has a massive impact on the way we feel. Changing your physiology is the quickest way to get into a useful state – physically act 'as if' you are feeling a certain way and you will actually start to feel that way, in other words:

Fake it to make it.

The powerful thing about physiology is that it affects other people too – remember that the appearance of achievement leads to achievement. Imagine this. Your company is launching a new product. Your CEO kicks off a launch event to the whole company, to tell everyone how proud he is of the new product. He ambles slowly on to the stage, looking at the floor. He fiddles nervously with his microphone and shifts from one foot to the other.

Hmmm, less believable than a politician talking about shortening NHS waiting lists. Why? He does not have a physiology of pride. Think about successful people you know, or successful people on the television. How do they hold themselves? Have a go at mimicking their physiology. Imagine you are Beckham walking on to the pitch as England's captain, imagine you are Robbie Williams in front of thousands of screaming fans. Whatever lights your candle – you can pretend to wear Wonder Woman's pants for all I care – just get into the physiology of being proud and you'll shoot up to a ten.

Another really simple way to tap into your pride is through visualisation. Read the next paragraph through and then do what it says:

Imagine a time when you were really proud – it doesn't matter why, it's just important that you felt really proud, strong and full of self-belief. Make the memory as real as possible. Imagine where you were – what could you see? What colours were there? What could you hear? Were there people talking to you? What were they saying? What could you feel? Can you remember what you were wearing? How were you breathing? Step into the picture, become fully associated – imagine you are really there, it is happening now.

Close your eyes and run that imagination exercise right now.

How did the exercise make you feel? The chances are you recaptured that feeling of pride and brought it to the here and now.

The next step is to set up an anchor or trigger, so you can magic up that feeling of pride in an instant. Repeat the visualisation exercise and this time, as the feeling of pride becomes stronger and stronger make some form of action – for example clench your thumb in your fist, and think of a colour. The more you do this, the stronger the link will be between the feeling of pride and the anchor you have set up. You will find that soon all you need to do is fire off the anchor and you will access your feeling of pride in an instant.

The Sin of
ENVY

'In a consumer society there are inevitably two kinds of slaves –
the prisoners of addiction and the prisoners of envy'.

Ivan Illich

'In Belmarsh Jail, there are two kinds of prisoners –
the prisoners of poverty and my husband.'

Mary Archer

THE SIN OF ENVY IS USUALLY DESCRIBED as that feeling of grudging or admiring discontent aroused by the possessions, achievements or personal qualities of someone else, which leads to the overwhelming desire to acquire what they have. It is portrayed by the Bible as a mean little sin, a sneering and viscous grub, eating away at the apple of contentment. It is, in short, the foundation stone of the consumer society. Every piece of advertising copy ever written assumes envy in the minds of the potential buyer.

'Look at my white wash! If only you had a washing machine like mine, your shirts would gleam like new!'
'What are you doing with that washing machine? It only has one drum, you poor, deprived thing.
My washing machine has two drums – can't you see what you're missing?'

*In all probability
he'd gladly let you
have the blonde for
the price of a lager
with lemonade*

And so we rush out and buy Mr Dyson's latest two-drum machine or his no-bag vacuum cleaner, even though there's absolutely nothing wrong with the items we bought only six months ago. For goodness sake, until recently men had to shave every morning with a razor that had only two blades. Can you imagine that? Then we saw that muscular hunk on the television with a blonde caressing his chin – a chin made smooth as silk by his three-blade engineering masterpiece – bingo! That's what we want. That's what we must have. The fact that it's actually his blonde girlfriend we want is a subconscious detail we've neatly overlooked. (As is the near certainty that smoothie-chin razor man is a gay out-of-work actor: 'The best a man can get'. In all probability he'd gladly let you have the blonde for the price of a lager with lemonade top.)

You've got the new washing machine, the best vacuum cleaner and a multi-blade safety razor. So, you sit in your gleaming shirt admiring your dust-free carpets as your blonde girlfriend gently caresses your stubble-free chin.

Has your sense of envy gone away?

Of course it hasn't.

Reclining in his leather armchair in a plush office in deepest Highbury, Arsène Wenger dials Alex Ferguson's mobile telephone number and waits for the Manchester United manager to answer. Alex picks up the call and they chat for a while. The weather's grim up north, Arsène discovers, but soothes Alex with the news that pints are more expensive down south. They debate which city offers the better standard of living. You can't buy a lock-up garage for less than half a million in the city, while a six-bedroomed mansion could be yours for the price of a second-hand car in Cheadle Hulme. The Arndale Centre is a bit grim, whereas the Tate Modern is a fine facility. Talk turns to their respective families. Alex says how delighted he is to hear that Arsène's wife and kids have adjusted well to life in London and Arsène reminds Alex he hasn't yet seen Alex's daughter's recent wedding photos.

Eventually, the pleasantries and idle chit-chat come round to the topic of football. Arsène wishes Alex good luck for Saturday. He tells Alex he'll be keeping his fingers crossed for the Manchester squad. Manchester United are at home to Arsenal.

The conversation swings to the subject of how Tottenham are getting on. Arsène and Alex agree that Glenn Hoddle has done a wonderful job with Arsenal's North London neighbours. He deserves success. He deserves recognition. He deserves to lift the League Cup.

So, Alex and Arsène hatch a plan. They will play their weakest sides, they will concede goals and throw games to push Glenn and his boys at Spurs into a position where they can hardly fail to win the League. Alex promises to ring round a few of his other manager mates and get them to collude. Arsène says that his best mate, Gerald Houllier, will be down from Liverpool visiting him that weekend and promises to have chat with the jolly Frenchman.

What absolute nonsense. Can you imagine it?

Envy drives competition.

Don't even think for a moment that Arsène Wenger, Alex Ferguson or any other football manager worth the job title would ever pass up the chance of getting their hands on the cup. They would sell their children for it. They would eat their own legs while sticking needles in their ears for it. Why? Because they want that cup. They want that success. Arsenal, Spurs and Liverpool don't come to cosy arrangements to lose because they want what, for the last few seasons, Manchester United have had. And what Manchester United have had, they guard with envy's right-hand man – jealousy.

'Jealousy is the green-eyed monster which doth mock the meat it feeds on.'
William Shakespeare

'Have you forgotten to take your Prosac again?'
William Shakespeare's doctor

All truly successful sports team managers use envy as a weapon to spur their players on to better performance levels. They want to join the elite in Europe. They want to play at Wembley or Cardiff. They want to have their matches broadcast on Skysports. They want to finish top of the league. They want to knock Manchester United off their perch, or even better, be on a perch higher above them.

Do you settle for a life of second-bests? Are you proud to tell your partner that you sold less than your work colleague? Does the phrase 'It's not the winning that counts, it's the taking part' count in business?

Envy – the desire to be where the top dog is.

Football players are envious of each other. A dozen goalies want to be net-minder for England. Only one can get the job. Thirty premier league strikers dream of scoring for their country. The manager selects just two. Envy, the desire for other's status, drives each player to train harder, to play harder, to work harder, to push himself further and faster.

Ignore what the Church says about envy. Envy is one of the strongest self-motivation tools in the box.

Think of it like this. What is the difference between playing for Nottingham Forest and playing for Liverpool? About thirty thousand a week. But apart from that, is there really that much difference between their strikers? Partly it's about ability, but probably only by a very slim margin. The real difference is the desire to be a champion. The aspiration to acquire to a champion's skills and, probably even more of a spur, the champion's spoils.

Paul Scholes knows he is a champion. He has pride, the sense of self-worth that tells him he's a champion. But Patrick Vieira thinks he's better than Scholes. Patrick believes he can tackle harder, cross more accurately, keep the ball longer and hit the back of the net more frequently than any other player in the Premier League. Patrick Viera wants to win a trophy. Why? Because he views Scholes and Manchester United through eyes sharpened with envy. He wants to be top dog.

Envy doesn't just allow you to set goals. It lets you know when you've scored them.

The world of business is very similar to the world of football. In the case of Manchester United, it's very nearly indistinguishable. There is little to differentiate the top Chief Executive from the middle of the road Chief Executive. They both know how to do their job, and to the untrained eye probably do exactly the same job in exactly the same way. They both have the same skills. The difference is the desire for status, for recognition.

There is an old story about the man who claims to know every single person in the world. Let's call him Harry Palmer. A good mate, of whom obviously Harry has many, doesn't quite believe this claim and so bets Harry a thousand pounds that he can't prove he knows everyone in the world.

Harry duly drives his pal to Downing Street, and as they pass by, Tony and Cherie lean out of the window, wave and call out 'Hello Harry!' As they go round the corner into the Mall, the Queen passes by in an open carriage. 'Good morning Harry!' she

SAINT OR SINNER?

In eighteenth-century Europe, having tall people in your retinue was essential for the monarch about town. No one took this as seriously as Frederick William 1 of Prussia (1688–1740), however, who was so obsessed with having the tallest retinue of all, that he formed a regiment called the Potsdam Guards in which only the tallest men could serve. But William envied the taller soldiers of other nations and would risk war to have them. An Irishman called Kirkhman was kidnapped from the streets of London for £1000 and a tall monk was taken from Italy in the middle of Mass.

calls. They stop at traffic lights next to a police car. A window is wound down, 'Hi, Harry! Kids all right?' ask the two constables within. And so on. Every person they come across in London seems to know Harry Palmer. 'Okay,' says Harry's betting pal, 'you might know everyone in London, in England even, but what about abroad? I bet you don't know the Pope'.

They fly to Rome. The Alitalia pilot comes on the tannoy, tells them what the weather over the Alps is doing, gives an ETA at Fiumicino, wishes everyone a pleasant flight and says hello to his old friend Harry Palmer. At the Vatican, Harry explains that he'll pop in to see John Paul, but his pal will have to watch from outside as they're picky about who's allowed in. 'Fair enough', says the pal, 'Bring the Pope out on the balcony above St Peter's Square, and I'll see the two of you together, if you really know him.' Sure enough, Harry appears on the papal balcony, chatting and embracing his friend Pope John Paul II.

Harry's pal is incredulous and, staring the imminent loss of a quick grand in the face, tries to catch Harry out. So he turns to the Italian worshiper next to him and says 'Do you know who that bloke is up there?' and the Italian replies: 'I'm not sure about the one in the funny hat, but the other one's Harry Palmer.'

No one remembers a runner-up. Champions are etched in our memory and saluted for their efforts. Who would you rather be?

Envy is the desire for recognition.

The distinction between a merely good salesman and a truly great salesman isn't skill. They've both been on the same sales courses, both been taught the same skills at the same chain hotel just outside Reading. They've both picked up the same skills, have both honed the same tricks of the trade. The difference that marks out one from the other is attitude. The champion salesman wants to be the company's top salesman, and because he wants the title so badly, he will keep the title until a new champion comes along with a stronger desire to be the best.

We are taught by the Bible to perceive envy as a negative attribute. Christianity tells us it is the nastiest, ugliest, meanest and grimmest of the Seven Deadly Sins. Chaucer, who was writing in a time when religion was the only political system known, calls it 'a foul sin. . . the worst there is'. Hardly surprising really, considering the possible repercussions to the poet from the benevolant dictatorship that is the Church.

If Chaucer had written 'Envy is good. It will drag you from the treadmill of serfdom, slavery and poverty', he would have been hanged, drawn and quartered. In those days they didn't even have the decency to wait until you were dead, before getting out the quartering knives. Chaucer may have been a bit of an air-headed storyteller, but he wasn't stupid.

So, could this relentless selling of envy as bad be because the Church doesn't want us to realise our full potential? Does it suit the Church for us settle for second place at best, not to reach our earthly destiny? Certainly, there must be a danger that if we all get everything we want, we won't need to pray for anything. And if we don't need to pray, we won't need a god to pray to.

Of all the commercially developed Western nations, the United States is undoubtedly the most successful in terms of material standards of living. Generally, a high level of religious observance is associated with poor nations. Not unnaturally, people who live a miserable life here on earth look to some improvement in the next world. However, the United States has one of the highest rates of religious observance of any nation. This would appear to debunk the theory that sins such as envy are foisted upon us to keep us down, knowing our place, to stop us from trying to find a way out of poverty.

However, the vast majority of regular churchgoers are comprised of the black, Hispanic and other non-white minorities. In short, the poor. It is true to say that some very successful, high-profile, white Americans profess to religious observance. Bill Clinton was to be seen taking prayers with his personal minister every breakfast time, but only after he'd used his wealth, power and position to commit seedy little acts of adultery over which the moral majority of the electorate might otherwise have become outraged if he hadn't atoned. In the southern states, the notorious Bible Belt, where most of the white church-goers will be found, sin-avoidance is at best selective and certainly rooted in hypocrisy. The southern states fought a war in their attempt to retain slavery, and have never forgiven the north for taking victory. There are still those who routinely plant a burning cross, the very symbol of their Christian faith, to warn black transgressors of their white moral code of the fate they have in store. They try to force their black neighbours to understand the Sin of Envy in a similar fashion to the Church itself.

Bill Clinton was to be seen taking prayers with his personal minister every breakfast time, but only after he'd used his wealth, power and position to commit seedy little acts of adultery over which the moral majority of the electorate might otherwise have become outraged if he hadn't atoned.

We teach our children that winning isn't important,
it's the taking part that counts.

Does that make any sense? Is the world too politically correct?

Envy as a sin teaches us that we don't have the right to obtain anything. When Emmeline Pankhurst founded the Women's Social and Political Union in 1903, her movement was regarded as an expression of envy simply because she wanted certain

THE SIN OF ENVY – BURGER KING

Burger King has made no secret of its envy. It has made it an explicit corporate goal to overtake its nemesis, McDonald's, within five years. It wants to be the number one in the burger game and it's going to do everything in its power to get there.

Burger King already has more than 11,000 restaurants worldwide, selling nearly two billion flame-grilled Whoppers every year. For a long while, its burgers were often rated ahead of McDonald's but its French fries were always marked lower. So Burger King set its sights on wiping out the deficit and spent millions developing a new super fry. It looks to be working.

Rest assured, wherever the Burger King Corporation has identified a weakness vis-à-vis McDonalds it will close the gap in its envy-fuelled crusade to claim the crown it so desperately desires.

rights for women that men already had. At that time, women who entered into marriage were forced by law to leave their jobs. Women who were beaten by their husbands were forced by law to stay in the marriage. Women didn't have the vote.

The Suffragette's 'want list' wasn't a long one, nor was it unreasonable, and yet its aims were summed up as envy. Failing to find a good argument against votes for women, envy was the best counter-argument the establishment could manage. And yet, so all-pervasive was the fear of sinning, that women in their millions prayed in church every Sunday for the souls of poor, deluded Mrs Pankhurst and her sinning sisters.

Envy prevents you being satisfied with second place.

Does that make it a sin?

Certainly, envy can be a nasty little sin if it leads to an air of resignation. It can work against you, but only if you believe what religion says. Used properly, envy makes us more competitive, both within ourselves and against others. It makes us try harder, go the extra mile. It turns us into champions.

There is a story from ancient Greece about a man who killed himself through envy of another citizen of his city-state. We learn that the City Fathers decided to erect a statue in honour of a renowned local athlete who had brought them fame and honour through his prowess and success. Our man of envy was also an athlete, but

S A I N T   O R   S I N N E R ?

Sigmund Freud, a man who might be considered an expert on such matters, confessed to committing the Sin of Envy on numerous occasions. None was more famous than his envy of Albert Einstein. Jealousy, on this occasion, was invoked by what Sigmund perceived to be Einstein's easy route to success. He wrote to the Nobel-winning scientist on his fiftieth birthday, congratulating him and reminding Einstein that he, Freud, was 25 years older.

Einstein responded, 'Although you may have slipped into the skins of so many people, and even of mankind itself, you have had no opportunity of slipping into mine!'

Fortunately for Freud, he was in the position to defend his sin 'Envy need not be something ugly. Envy can include admiration and is reconcilable with the friendliest feeling for the person envied,' he replied.

had always played second fiddle to this champion. He was being eaten away inside at the thought of the people of the city admiring the statue and thinking of their great sporting hero. He wanted his own face on that statue, his body standing on that mighty Doric plinth, his head adorned by the laurel wreath of victory.

But it wasn't his statue, so he decided he would destroy it. Each night under the cover of darkness, he went down to the city square with hammer and chisel and took a small piece of stone away from the base of the statue. Using only hand tools, this was to be a lengthy process, but he stuck at it, night after night, until months later, having chiselled away a small piece every night, the statute finally fell. He would never have to put up with seeing that statue being admired ever again, because it fell on top of our man and crushed him to death. The athlete took the

SAINT OR SINNER?

Writers and philosophers seem to be those most likely to benefit from the Sin of Envy. As seventeenth-century English poet John Gay says, 'Envy's a sharper spur than pay, no author ever spared a brother, wits are gamecocks to one another.' And the literary world is littered with defences of envy: Petrarch was accused of being rather chilly in his criticism of Dante's masterpiece, *The Inferno*, because of envy – which he denied in letters. But eighteenth-century wit Lady Mary Wortley Montagu didn't bother to defend her envy of her competitors Swift and Pope. Instead, she had a lavatory bowl decorated with their faces so she could defecate on them every day.

Lady Mary Wortley Montagu didn't bother to defend her envy of her competitors Swift and Pope. Instead, she had a lavatory bowl decorated with their faces so she could defecate on them every day.

power of envy and misused it. He should instead have walked past the statute every day and used it as a talisman to spur him to try harder.

Just being the best isn't good enough – ask Betamax.
Success requires more than just talent.
It needs a naked desire to be a winner.

Envy is the driving force of market competition.

My father was a very good businessman, and he became very good and stayed very good by working very hard. Because he worked so hard, he was never around when I was growing up. I was envious of my friends' relationships with their fathers. Not because they had a relationship and I didn't, but because of the benefits that these relationships brought my friends. They and their fathers played tennis together, they went fishing together and later, went on boys' nights out together. I aspired to that kind of father and son relationship, which would have given me all those things with my father. When my father finally retired, we learned golf together. Now that I'm a father, I aspire to be the kind of father other children will be envious of.

S A I N T   O R   S I N N E R ?

Pepsi want one thing, and one thing only; to be the world's leading soft drink. Nothing else matters to the company that has been forced to play second fiddle to Coke for as long as the black fizzy stuff has been on supermarket shelves. And, considering how powerful the name 'Coke' has become (some would go so far as to say that Coke stands for everything that is American), Pepsi have performed a miracle of their own in keeping up.

The burning sense of envy at Pepsi has been an endless source of motivation, driving it to take aim at Coke's dominance from every conceivable angle. Rumour has it that the word 'Coke' is banned at Pepsi HQ!

Pepsi have even been known to fire ad agencies for drinking Coke instead of their precious cola. A consultant from a top public relations agency told me of a panic that spread through their agency when they ordered a take-away half-way through a client meeting with Pepsi. The pizza came with a free bottle of Coke. The restaurant was never used again.

Such envy has even spurred 'cola advertising wars' with the two brands fighting it out to employ the trendiest, most popular celebrities to endorse their products. It's a battle Pepsi seems to be winning, with a line-up ranging from football players to popstars.

What makes the difference between a father – merely the male parent – and good father? In part, it is the application of skills. You need to know how to change nappies. You need to know when to exercise discipline, when to exercise latitude. You need to know when to dangle carrots and when to bring out the rod. More than that, a good father wants to give his son everything he never had when he was a child. He's envious of those things the other kids had when he was child, and wants to give those things to his own child.

This is why members of the British Royal Family make such terrible parents. What was there that the other kids had, that they didn't, that might spur them on to make good parents? A new polo pony? A private train? A medium-sized county with fishing rights? India? The only thing they never had, that other children did, was rickets. And they probably never actually met any of them. What can they possibly be envious of? These very few people haven't committed the sin of envy because they can't think of anything to be envious of. They're not sinners, they're lazy. Filthy rich and lazy, admittedly.

A good father wants to give his son everything he never had when he was a child. He's envious of those things the other kids had when he was a child... This is why members of the British Royal Family make such terrible parents

Envy is ambition.
Envy provides a measuring stick to see how well you can do.
Envy is good for you.

There is no shame in envy.

Ask anyone to name a car-hire firm and they will say Avis or Hertz. A lot of them will also insist on telling the joke about Hertz Van Rental being a striker for Ajax. Hertz is the largest vehicle rental company in the world, with representation in over 140 countries. A second-hand car dealer in Chicago invented the self-drive car-hire system in 1918. He noted the many men returning from the First World War, and the immigrants arriving by the shipload from Europe, who had been trained to drive in the army.

With the rapid expansion of the US economy and a massive movement of peoples across the country from east to west, Chicago was an ideal location to take advantage of a previously unheard-of concept. Bought by John D. Hertz in 1923, who quickly renamed the company in his own honour, it soon had offices at railway stations, was the first to operate at airports and then the first to go international.

By 1946, Hertz had been bought out again, this time by General Motors. As the corporation that eventually took the crown as the world's largest motor manufacturer from Henry Ford, GM is still not just the world's largest car maker, but arguably the world's largest company in any field.

Strangely, for a car maker, GM's name rarely appears on its cars. They make Buicks, Chevrolets, Pontiacs, Vauxhalls and Opels, they even make Frigidaire appliances, but they don't make 'GM' anythings. The only other major car maker who never put their name on their cars was British Leyland, and who can blame them for keeping quiet?

Even back in 1946 General Motors was a Goliath with massive financial clout, when a David, in the form of Avis, appeared on the scene. Avis weren't just the underdog, they weren't even a flea on the backside of the underdog. They were nowhere. But they grew, and by the time their advertising agency devised their motto 'We try harder', they were still down in sixth place in the pecking order of car rental firms.

'We try harder' has since become the fifth most famous line in advertising history and Avis are now second in size only to Hertz. The campaign demonstrated naked corporate envy. Avis wanted what Hertz had. Avis wanted to be as big as Hertz. Avis wanted to be as successful as Hertz. Avis' cars were the same as Hertz. They were just as reliable or luxurious and were available at the same places at the same price as Hertz. So how could they be better? The advertising campaign told customers that Avis were so intent in becoming market leaders, their service would be superior to that provided by Hertz. 'We try harder' has become the spirit of Avis, so much so, in fact, that they now outstrip Hertz in customer loyalty surveys. They have gone from nowhere to second to the largest in the world simply through trying harder, and all thanks to envy. They aspire to be number one and they will probably make it.

Are you an Avis?
Who do you admire most? Why?

What have they got that you haven't got?

The Ten Commandments
of committing the sin of

ENVY

1 Envy provides goals.

All large successful companies are envious of what their competitors have. It might be customers, profits or product sales. The major petrol retailers measure their sales success almost entirely on market share. That is; not 'How well are we doing?' but rather; 'How well are we doing compared to the others?' If they are below a competitor in the market-share league, they look to take that share. During the petrol price wars of the 1960s and 1970s, oil companies even posted look-outs with binoculars on high buildings to monitor how their competitor retail-site pump prices were moving and reacted instantly.

2 Let envy motivate.

How do you know what you want if you've never seen it? We're not all Thomas Edisons or George Stephensons. We're not going to invent the next unheard of item of equipment that will change the world and turn us into millionaires overnight. So be shamelessly envious of what others have got, and be motivated by it.

As a teenage boy, a friend of mine was cycling to school one day when he saw a car. Not just any car, but a Shelby AC Cobra 427. He had never seen one before. He didn't know what it was. Up until that point, he didn't know he wanted one. All he knew was that now he really wanted one. As soon as he left school and started earning money, he began saving to buy the car, but quickly realised that if he worked every day of his life, lived to be ninety years old and saved every penny he had, he still wouldn't have enough cash to buy a Shelby AC Cobra 427. So what he did he do? Did he resign himself to driving a second-hand Datsun Cherry? No, he didn't. He gave up his office job and went to work as an apprentice in a motor repair garage on an even lower salary. He stayed late at the workshop, where he could use the lathes and the spanners and the welders for free. On behalf of the garage, he ordered a workshop manual for 427 Cobra from Shelby. He refurbished second-hand parts from crash repairs and scrapped cars. He learnt how to fashion bodywork by watching the panel beaters, and he made an exact copy at a fraction of the price of the real thing.

3 Never satisfy your envy.

Make your envy insatiable by always looking to the next object of your desire. Don't confuse satisfaction with complacency. When my friend had finished building his Shelby AC Cobra 427, he still had a problem. He wanted to drive it, but aged only nineteen, he couldn't afford to insure it. There was no way he was going to think about taking a backwards glance at the Datsun Cherry option.

Being a law-abiding type, he wasn't about to drive around uninsured – well certainly not in a police magnet like a 427 Cobra. So he changed jobs again. This time he became an insurance clerk. As an employee of a reputable firm of underwriters, he could approve his own insurance rating and calculate his own premium, one that he could easily afford on his meagre clerk's wages. The premium would otherwise have been the equivalent of more than a year's salary. If he'd simply sat back and admired his handiwork on the car, he'd have had nothing more than a nice ornament and a badly paid job. As it was, envy allowed him to drive one of the most gorgeous cars ever made.

4 Use envy as a spur to innovation.

The retail petrol sales manager eyeing his competitors' prices through his binoculars eventually turned his Peeping Tom acts to even better use. On the Thursday evening before Easter, he was gazing round the town from his perch and realised that every time he put his prices down to beat a particular competitor, his foe would immediately go a half-penny a gallon below him.

There are two things to remember about the Easter holiday in petrol retailing terms. As the first bank holiday of the year, with the kids out of school and workers taking a long weekend, it is the first big peak on the year's sales graph. The second thing is that no tanker deliveries will be made after 6 pm on Thursday until, at the earliest, 8 am on the following Tuesday. Most large forecourts have just about sufficient storage-tank capacity to cope with four days of heavy sales, but it can be marginal.

Binocular man, realising that his competitor was doing exactly the same trick as himself, fought back. He reduced his prices by a massive amount, to below cost and watched as his competitor's prices went a half-penny below that. Then he closed all his petrol stations in the town, but left all the lights on. In a sales rush lasting only a few hours, his competitor sold his entire stock, at a loss, and was as dry a bone for the entire holiday weekend. As the 'sold out' signs went up, binocular-man re-opened his sites, with the prices back up as high as possible, and happily sold good profitable fuel all weekend.

5 Envy everything you can.

Meanwhile, Cobra Man is getting a bit older. He feels his small flat is no longer sufficient for his needs. Driving through a nice part of the countryside one day in his pride and joy, he notices that a house he always liked the look of is up for sale. He has admired the nicely landscaped grounds, the tastefully restored Georgian brickwork and the ivy-clad barn. He is envious again. He knows the property is out of his price league, and that he doesn't even have the deposit, but what the hell, why not go in and have a look round? He drives through the gates, falling hopelessly in love with the house.

As he's parking on the gravel by the front door, the house owner comes out and says 'What a fantastic car. I've always wanted one of those'. He doesn't know it's not the real thing, doesn't even care, he wants it anyway. The problem of the deposit is solved. The house was Cobra Man's, or as he now was, ex-Cobra Man, subject to making the mortgage repayments. Sadly, he no longer had his car, and he had a house that was in danger of being repossessed if he didn't make the monthly payment. How did he solve those two problems? He started making replicas of his car in the large barn that came with the house. He sold them at a good profit and got his own new one free every year.

He is now one of the largest manufacturers of high performance sports cars in the UK. And he can afford to drive the real thing now.

6 Your envy is your potential.

We all have potential. The problem rests with trying to identify in which areas our potential should best be realised. The man who made his fortune from cultured pearls started out as a noodle maker. Kokichi Mikimoto was a Japanese peasant who inherited a noodle-making business from his father, who became ill and unable to work. At the age of just eleven Mikimoto now had to support the entire family, and so quickly expanded into sales as well as manufacture to raise extra income.

By the time he was in his twenties, he was very successful noodle maker and marketer, and started to move in higher social circles. He met and fell in love with the daughter of a Samurai. It wouldn't matter if Mikimoto had opened a chain of noodle restaurants in every capital city in the world; noodle making simply wasn't considered a trade for the future son-in-law of a Samurai. Mikimoto realised this without needing to be told. So he sold his business and became a pearl dealer. The sooner he became successful at that, the sooner he would get the bride. He envied the suave young men with their beautiful wives who moved serenely in their society circle and wanted to join them fast.

7 Envy puts no limit on potential.

Finding pearls was, until Mikimoto's time, a hit-and-miss affair, reliant on the vagaries of Mother Nature. He'd made things before, noodles admittedly, but even his finest high-grade rice spaghetti was hardly likely to be made into earrings to adorn fine ladies at the Japanese court, but why not make pearls? Everyone knew that pearls are created when a grain of sand becomes stuck in a oyster, but this doesn't happen in every oyster. The waste of effort in gathering every oyster, for the one in a hundred that contained a pearl, was what made them have such added value. Mikimoto bought himself an oyster bed, one from a pearl trader who had failed because his bed was so unproductive, and simply put a grain of sand into every oyster. Cultured pearls were born.

8 Envy eliminates opposition.

Soap rivals Unilever and Proctor & Gamble have such envy to be number one in the whiter wash league that they have, between them, spent in excess of $60 billion (at current values) on advertising expenditure. For over fifty years they have both eyed the number one spot. In the course of the biggest soap war in history, they have eliminated virtually all other competition. One or the other of these two makes every packet of soap powder adorning the supermarket shelves the world over.

9 Don't just envy success.

Think of the down and out person in the street, holding a grubby scrap of cardboard with the scrawl 'hungry and homeless'. Envy him. Why? He doesn't have to worry about meeting his monthly mortgage payments. His BMW isn't going to be vandalised by a bunch of mindless vandals. He doesn't have to scrimp and save to find school fees. He doesn't have to get up in the morning to go to a boring job. All these can be envied. All of these can be yours. Admittedly, our tramp lets off a stench that would down a rancid donkey at fifty paces, but you don't have to envy that.

10 Envy sells.

Why do designers put their labels on the outside of clothing? Why do Barbour jackets have a big shiny badge that says 'Barbour' on the lapel? For the same reason that cars have mobile phone aerials on their roofs. To sell. During the explosion of car-phone sales in the late 1908s, manufacturers found their customers wanted to show off that they had the latest bit of yuppie technology. These phones didn't need an outside aerial. How many of us have taken ours off in preparation to go through the car wash, and forgotten all about it until two years later when we sold the car and found the aerial in the glove box? They are badges to show off, but more importantly for the manufacturers, they made other motorists envious. Other motorists wanted car phones. Actually they didn't. What they did want was the aerial.

One enterprising company made a small fortune selling dummy aerials, which, incidentally, they sold for more than the price of the real thing.

Exercise on

ENVY

You won't need to run through the exercises from the chapter on Pride to get into a state of envy, most of us are born with over-active envy glands. But envy is pointless and corrosive unless you do something about it. The cynics will claim there is no point acting on envy, there's too much of a gap between you and the person you're envious of. Nonsense. Envy spurs us to try harder.

Try this:

- Raise your arm in the air and stretch your hand as far as it will go.
- Now, put your arm down and shake it out.
- Now raise your arm again and this time stretch as far as it will go . . . and now even further.

Did your hand go higher the second time? I bet it did, just a fraction. Then why on earth didn't you stretch it that far the first time? The instruction was to 'stretch your hand as far as it will go'. At levels of peak performance there is a very small gap that separates first place from second. So what makes a difference? Your skill didn't change between the first and second attempt – your attitude did. The first step to effectively harnessing envy is having the attitude of a champion. We learned how to do that in pride.

The next step is to figure out how champions become champions – what is their recipe for success? One way of doing this is to go through years of effort, using a process of trial and error, to try and replicate what they've done. If that's your preferred approach, I suggest you throw this book away now. If you don't understand why, trust me, I'll explain when we get to the Sin of Sloth.

It's a lot easier to steal the recipe for success.

There was a programme on television not long ago about a chap who introduced Britain to 'proper sausages' – not the breadcrumbs-and-BSE stuff we'd been used to, but tasty posh combinations such as pork and leek, venison and cranberry, all supported by a secret blend of herbs and spices. They were a runaway success. He went from a small shop to a highly successful nationwide enterprise. Then disaster struck. One of his employees left, set up in competition and knocked the stuffing out of our hero's success. The original sausage maker is adamant that the only way his employee could have done this without years of trial and error was by stealing his recipes.

Am I suggesting that you grab a balaclava and a swag bag? No, there are far easier ways to steal a recipe.

Maybe it's ego, maybe it's generosity, but a lot of successful people give away their secrets for free. Go into any bookshop and I guarantee there'll be a book by someone you envy, full of advice and tips. Head for the autobiography section in particular. You may have to stomach patronising advice and bottom-clenchingly bad reminiscences 'Ah, dear Larry, I remember the time when . . .' but it is worth it.

Another really simple way is to ask people. If invention may be the mother of skill, flattery is the mother of damn-good-tips-it-would-have-taken-you-years-to-find-out. Let's say you are a salesman and you envy the top dog who always wins top salesperson of the year, the wide-screen television prize and the best seat in the office. Take them out for a beer, confess how you've always admired them, and ask for their autograph, whatever it takes to get them into a mellow frame of mind. Then shake your head, sigh and say 'You're so successful, I just don't know how you do it!' All you have to do now is sit back, smile, switch on the hidden Dictaphone and nod wistfully as they pour out all of their top tips.

In fact, you can learn loads without even asking. Successful people leave clues that even Inspector Clouseau could have picked up. Take that top salesman. Go on an undercover reconnaissance mission to piece together his recipes for success:

- Look at their diary – how do they spend their time? What do they do that you don't?
- What's in their bag? Do they have notebooks full of meeting notes? Do they carry loads of marketing bumf?
- How is their desk organised?
- Who do they know and who do they spend time with?
- How do they greet people? How do they walk into a room?
- What do they wear, what's their appearance like?

Am I suggesting that you become their clone, copying everything they do? No way. You envy their success, not their shoe size. Just remember that if you do what you've always done you'll get what you've always got. If you want different results you need to try something different. Well, here's your chance to go play. You envy their results, so try out their methods.

GLUTTONY

'They're overpaid, overfed, over-sexed and over here.'

Tommy Trinder, British comedian during the Second World War

'Thanks for the compliments.'

General Dwight D. Eisenhower, Commander US Army, Europe

WHEN GOD PUT IN A CALL TO HIS BESPOKE SIN-MAKER to have gluttony put on the list, the phone must have made the sound of a barrel being scraped. Having an extra few fries with your double quarter-pounder with cheese may put on a few pounds but it certainly doesn't sound much like a one-way ticket to hell.

In the minds of the religious, what lust is to sex, gluttony is to food. To regard eating too much as a mortal sin may have been a reasonable moral code at a time when, as a result of plagues of locusts and fleeing slavery in Egypt, people were starving to death, but when the world is producing enough food to feed us all to the point where we need to buy a larger waist size every few months, what could possibly be morally wrong with a good blow out now and again? True, there are still parts of the world with more than their fair share of under-fed people, but that is a problem of distribution rather than availability. Food not eaten in Surrey isn't going to help anyone in sub-Saharan Africa.

It was Groucho Marx who said that a healthy diet and no drinking doesn't make you live longer, it just makes it seem as if you're living a lot longer.

The Bible likens the glutton to the fat pig at the trough, his snout noisily chomping into as much fodder as possible in the shortest possible time. We still mock the overweight. We still frown at the fat person on the train eating a chocolate bar. We praise those who go to the gym every day, who drink no alcohol, who call half a lettuce leaf, a slice of cucumber and a carrot juice a three-course dinner. Despite being a nonsensical sin, it has got into our fabric. There are those who still believe that enough is as good as a feast.

It was Groucho Marx who said that a healthy diet and no drinking doesn't make you live longer, it just makes it seem as if you're living a lot longer. And it was Jack Dee who said that a healthy diet does provide a few extra years of life, but the wrong ones – who wants to live longer when all you can do is sit in a nappy looking out of window, speculating whether the man in the bed next to yours has died while waiting for the nurse to come round to wipe the dribble off your shirt? You want the extra years when you're fit enough to enjoy them.

Do you live life to the full or do you hold back?
Do you feast on life or are you on a diet?

The Sin of Gluttony teaches us to want a longer, fuller life.

Time is our only finite natural asset. You can't really do much to extend an active life. You can do quite a lot to shorten it, but the simple answer is not to light the barbecue using a gallon of unleaded and a blowlamp. If you can't extend the length of your life, then expand the capacity. Pack more into it. Pack everything you can into it. When you've packed in everything you possibly can, work out how to pack in some more. Get gluttonous.

There is one way to extend the length of a human's life that scientists have been working on for decades: the time-travel machine. This isn't a joke. Well-funded, well-educated senior scientists have, in recent years, cracked the theory of the problem of how to travel in time, so that at the age of fifty you can go back and be twenty-five again. Apparently, time travel only works one way, i.e., we can't go forwards, presumably because that time hasn't happened yet and there is nothing to visit. But they really believe that within a few centuries, time travellers will be going back to visit their long-dead ancestors. But let's not get too hung up on time travel. I am no scientist, but even I can figure out that if a time machine is going to work in the future then we would have seen one by now.

So let's assume we have to pack more into the same life-span.

Biblical gluttony focuses on food and the effect of taking in too much, too quickly and too noisily. I'm not about to propose that you go out and start overeating as an easy way to find overnight success, but our bodies do need food. They need a regular energy source. And so does the mind. You can have the best imagination in the world with the brainpower of several Einsteins, but if you don't feed it, it will wither and die. And the great thing about overfeeding the brain is that it doesn't get fat and flabby and slow. It has a near infinite capacity for information.

It is a provable scientific fact that we only
use 10% of our brainpower.

**Just imagine what we could achieve
if we used the other two-thirds.**

There is no such thing as useless information. There are no empty
calories in brain food. A friend of mine actually collects information the rest of us
would consider useless. He stores such fascinating facts as the name of the world's
tallest dwarf, the world's wettest desert and he knows that during the ice age there
was a species of bald, tuskless pygmy mammoths. He knows that traditional,
wooden umbrella handles are made out of Brussels sprout stalks and that there are
even varieties of sprout plants specially bred for umbrella-handle manufacture. He
knows that to make umbrella handles you need a supply of old telegraph poles.
(The sprouts are planted in straight rows and when they reach maturity, the leaves
and sprouts are stripped off, the stalks bent over the poles and tied to form the
shape. Then they are cut off at the base and left to dry. A coat of varnish, and there
you have a supply of umbrella handles.)

And I know what you're thinking now: 'Why should I want to know all this rubbish
about Brussels sprouts and telegraph poles?' The answer is that you probably don't.
It's too late. The man who discovered this was my friend's grandfather. After the last
war, Granddad was travelling across war-ravaged Europe in a jeep, picking his way
through the detritus strewn roads, and saw all sorts of stuff lying about, including
telegraph poles knocked down by the retreating German army. When he got home,

his father's farm was in trouble. It had been run intensively using the latest chemical technology to make as much food as possible for the war effort, but the soil was leeched out. In the harsh winter of 1946, the sprout crop grew long and straggly and produced virtually no sprouts worth the name.

During his time in the army, granddad shared officers' mess quarters with the Americans, who had much admired the traditions of the relatively old-fashioned British Army, including the officers' habit of carrying a neatly furled wooden-handled umbrella. He also spotted that during the war, everything in sight had been painted in Army Drab, khaki paint. Everything. Even beautifully crafted, wooden gun carriages, boat decks and transport vehicle dashboards. Before the war these had all been bulled up with shellac, an ancient form of varnish still used by antique furniture restorers. Granddad knew all these things. He didn't particularly want to know them, but when his family farm was about to go bust thanks to its spoilt soil and the terrible winter of 1946, he put all these facts together.

He went off with a farm lorry and trailer. He got the contract to clear away fallen telegraph poles. He was paid to take them away. He got the contract to clear away surplus stocks of shellac. The army had six years' worth of the stuff sitting in storage.

SAINT OR SINNER?

William Pitt the Younger, having been advised as a young man that it was good for his health to drink a bottle of port a day, took this advice on board. At one point he was drinking as much as six bottles of port, two of Madeira and one and a half of claret a day. He would throw up while making speeches in the Commons. Pitt the Younger was Prime Minister of England twice, from 1783 to 1801 and from 1804 to 1806.

They paid him to take it away. He put all these elements together, and sold traditional English umbrella handles to the only country in the world that could afford them – the United States.

His pals from the army who had returned to the States were going back into civilian businesses. They had shops and factories and outlets. Granddad made a fortune, simply by consuming every piece of knowledge he could and then putting them together in the right combination.

There were plenty of other people who knew about the fallen telegraph poles. There were thousands who saw piles of shellac in army quartermasters' stores. There were millions who worked on the land and watched crops ruined in the snow and ice of 1946. There were even more who knew what an umbrella handle looked like.

But they didn't all know all of these things.

Grandson has learned this lesson. He hasn't learnt how to use the information yet, but it is all certainly useful in the right place. Like here, in his friend's book, for example.

It's not just 'what you know' that counts.
It's not just 'who you know' that counts.

**It's 'what you know about who
you know' that counts.**

It's never too late to start the process of being a glutton for information. At the age of seventy-eight, and in happy retirement on a modest pension, Mr X (not his real name), decided to take a short holiday. In his working life, X had been an insurance clerk, working happily for a modest income right up until his retirement. When he packed in the job and took the gold watch at age sixty-five, he had time on his hands. And on his wrist, in fact. He did a bit of gardening, he repainted the kitchen and put up new tiles in the bathroom, but then, worried his brain was starting to waste away through lack of use, he started reading. He read everything and anything. Books, magazines, newspapers and comics. He just wanted to exercise the mind. He became a glutton for it.

Without listing every piece of useless information that Mr X had absorbed, you won't be surprised to hear that because of a delay to his holiday flight he turned £3000 into £50,000 in a matter of a few days.

British manufacturing industry failed during the 1950s and 1960s. Yes, I know some of it kept going, but how much is left now? Britain has service industries, component-assembly businesses and the tourist industry. There is precious little that Britain actually makes now, compared to the first half of the twentieth century.

During his reading sessions, Mr X developed an interest in this decline of British engineering excellence, but had no thought of using it to his financial advantage until he found himself stuck at the airport for three hours. He wandered off to the observation lounge to do a bit of plane spotting and saw something else. There was a gang of men knocking down a line of old hangars. The hangars were made of aluminum sheets. They were painted, but he could tell they were aluminum, one of

SAINT OR SINNER?

A bottle of Chateau Pétrus Vintage Claret will set you back around £10,000 at Gordon Ramsay's central London Pétrus restaurant. But when you're a successful 'city gent', charging your lunch to the company, such perks can be enjoyed – and then some. In July 2001 six successful sinners consumed three bottles of the Chateau Pétrus (the '45, '46 and '47, in case you were wondering) and several other bottles of rather pricey plonk, bringing their bill in at £7300 a head – and beating the previous record, held by a group of slightly less successful sinners, dining at Le Gavroche in 1997, of £4360 per person.

the lightest of metals, by the way two men could easily carry huge pieces. So he wandered off again and found the airport engineering facilities manager. 'What are you doing with those hangars?' he asked. The answer was that they were going for scrap. X offered three thousand pounds for the lot, on condition the airport would deliver the scrap to a UK seaport. He had a deal.

In various magazines, X had read about German car manufacturers experimenting with aluminum bodies. Their problem was that new aluminum isn't as malleable as old aluminum. The technology for pressing car bodies out of aluminum was in its infancy. Later, malleable alloys would be developed, but at that stage, if you wanted to press it, it had to be old. 1950's English aluminum was extremely high grade. No one in their right mind would construct buildings out of it, even to house jetliners. But Britain did in the 1950s.

X made one phone call to Germany. He sold the lot, for £50,000. His thirst for reading and his hungry bored mind had put disparate pieces of information together at a profit.

To put these various bits of information together, you need to know them first. The problem is that you don't know which you'll need until after you've got them all. But since you've only been using less than 10% of your brain to store everything you've seen, heard, learnt or thought about since birth, don't worry, there's plenty of spare storage space.

That's why you have to be a glutton.

THE SIN OF GLUTTONY – BP

As if it wasn't already big enough, British Petroleum went out and bought a couple more oil outfits to haul itself further up the league table to become the third largest integrated oil business in the world. Not bad for something that had been a state-run company until the 1980s.

Chief Executive John Browne, one of the most highly respected businessmen of his generation, presided over the hugely ambitious acquisition of US oil giant Amoco in 1998 and then the smaller but still strategically significant Atlantic Richfield Company (ARCO). The result is a massive production capacity.

On the downstream side of the business, BP operates no fewer than 29,000 petrol stations; runs one of the biggest petrochemical and specialty chemical manufacturers; and has recently expanded yet further by snapping up Burmah Castrol.

The success of this gluttonous strategy has been amply reflected by the company's share price, which generally responds far more enthusiastically to oil price movements than that of some of BP's other big competitors. The markets believe in BP's strategy and gluttony in a way that they haven't in some of its big competitors like, for example, Royal Dutch Shell.

Feast on news. Dine on information. Gorge on gossip.

The gluttonous know it is impossible to overdose on knowledge.

The most unlikely people are information gluttons. Working in the offices of a major multinational during the early 1970s was an elderly, lowly messenger. He used to deliver the mail around the offices and was a nice chatty type who, quite subliminally, had picked up all sorts of information simply by inadvertently eavesdropping on conversations. He had a better overall view of what was going on in the oil world than any department manager or regional co-ordinator. Because he went into most of the offices most weeks, he couldn't help but pick up this information. Then one Friday evening in 1973, he picked up a phone and bought a cargo of Saudi Light crude oil. Not a huge cargo – just a small VLCC load of about 100,000 tonnes.

On Monday afternoon he sold it. The price had gone up by $7 dollars a barrel. There are about eight barrels to the tonne of Saudi Light. He made a gross profit of $5.6 million.

Too good to be true? Yes. The elderly 'messenger' was in fact a retired oil rep who had returned to work after his wife had died, just to get himself out of a lonely house. He had intended only to work as a messenger for the companionship, but quickly noticed that no other job in the business allowed such a free supply of information. He learned in one office that a Middle East war was about to kick off. He learned in another that the market traders, unaware of an impending war, were looking at prices going down due to oversupply. He learned in the accounts section that oil trades have a 30-day settlement period, so he didn't have to lay out any cash. He heard in another office that 'If ever there was another Middle East war, crude would go up by at least $5 a barrel'. The mistake he made was telling a senior department manager over a Friday lunchtime pint in the pub, rather than just quietly taking the plunge. He committed the Sin of Gluttony to perfection. He failed to commit the Sin of Avarice.

The manager left his job that very afternoon and pocketed $5.6 million on Monday evening. What the messenger didn't know was that the manager was an inveterate gambler, to the extent that he was about to lose everything over a unsettled debt. Within a week he would have been bankrupt. He literally had nothing to lose.

That manager knew about gluttony; he had worked in the oil business for twenty years, and the major oil companies are the biggest corporate gluttons in the commercial world. They take in everything.

The more knowledge you consume,
the more knowledgeable you become.
The more competition you consume,
the more competitive you become.

You are what you eat.

THE SIN OF GLUTTONY – RENTOKIL

Rentokil's gluttony is legendary. It started out as a pest-control business and has evolved over the years into a giant provider of business services. Its reach within the sector is now phenomenal, with representation in every corner of its market. It is involved in everything from industrial cleaning, pest control and property-care services, to electronic surveillance, resort management and textiles.

Its voraciousness became one of the defining features of the firm under Chief Executive Clive Thompson, who earned himself the moniker of 'Mr Ten Per Cent' because he promised that sort of appreciation in the share price every year, a record he maintained until 1999.

The company describes its present strategy as searching for 'bolt-on acquisitions' in its core areas, in the UK, Europe and the United States. It has swallowed whole many of its competitors in the process of expanding and now boasts around 100,000 employees in more than 40 countries. Its latest acquisition was the Danish firm Ratin, which had owned 32% of the firm.

Look at any list of the world's largest companies, no matter how that might be measured and, for best part of a century, it will constantly include the major oil companies up there at the top.

Look at any list of the world's largest companies, no matter how that might be measured and, for best part of a century, it will constantly include the major oil companies up there at the top. This has been done through gluttony.

In most businesses, there are many different companies involved along the supply chain. Not in the gluttonous world of oil. Originally, the oil majors owned the oil fields. (Many are still owned this way, but increasingly in recent years host governments have muscled in.) They own the oil reserves. They own the oilrigs and derricks. They own the pipelines and the tankers that move the oil to the refineries, which they own. They own the downstream distribution systems, they own the petrol stations and the airport refuellers and the road tankers and . . . they own the lot. They even own things they don't want. Gluttony makes you fat, does it? Oil companies like being fat. Fat equals fat everything – including profits.

Most conventional business wisdom tells us we have to be mean, fit and lean to be profitable.

Rubbish. Top class, steaming pile of pony, rubbish.

In a normal supply chain, A digs up the raw material. He sells it at a profit. B moves the raw material on his trucks, at a profit. C takes the material into his factory and makes it into commodity, at a profit. D buys the commodity and makes it into products, at a profit. E moves the products to the shops, at a profit. F sells the products in his shops, at a profit. That's six profits in a very simple supply chain. The oil majors own all of these and more.

On this very simple model they make six profits in a row. But more than that, they swallow up bits of the supply chain they don't even need. Why? To stop the competition getting it. To stop the middleman. Oil companies don't like middlemen – they're like worms in the stomach. Worms make you thin, and thin equals thin profit.

Of course, there are business gurus who will argue against corporate gluttony. 'Specialise in one thing!' they'll cry. 'Do what you do best. Hire in the experts'.

Nonsense. Every business can expect one of four things to happen at some stage in their lifetime; they can go bust, they can stay as they are, they can get taken over, or they can acquire other companies. As long as you don't consume too much, too quickly (don't overstretch yourself) there's not a valid argument against corporate gluttony.

In its heyday, a major oil company which will remain nameless, but as a hint they use a shell as their logo, would regularly advertise in the press for applications for a job. One single opening. They might get a hundred applicants. Oil companies used to pay well, and there was high interest amongst the aspiring yuppie classes. Of those hundred applicants, they would whittle the best down to say, fifty for interview. Then they would take on the best twenty – for one job. Why? To stop the competition getting them. If someone doing a normal day's work can sell a million bucks worth of oil a day (which is quite normal) even his inflated salary gets lost in the second decimal of the price of a gallon of four star. And so do those of the other nineteen.

That's gluttony in action.

But the oil majors don't just restrict themselves to owning everything to do with the oil business. They own banks, pension funds and insurance companies. They make profits on these and get free banking, pensions and no insurance premiums. They do their own designing and printing of stationery. They paint their own road vehicles. They do everything. They even employ people to sit about all day thinking about what they don't do, to make sure they don't miss anything. For every oil rep out on the road there are two analysts sitting in an office just thinking and absorbing every piece of information they can find. You never know what might be useful, so have it all.

SAINT OR SINNER?

Jeffrey Bernard was one of Fleet Street's most highly regarded columnists despite a ravenous appetite for booze which saw him even more well known in the drinking establishments of Soho than in the dailies. His by-line would regularly read 'Jeffrey Bernard is unwell' to account for the occasions on which he was too drunk to submit copy. This phrase became immortalised in the title of a play about him by his long-time friend, Keith Waterhouse, starring Peter O'Toole. A great man, with an even greater thirst.

There's a joke about Luciano Pavarotti, the fine Italian opera tenor and lard mountain. On a trip to London, he sees a sign outside a small booth, which reads, '"Speak your weight" machine'. Luciano's command of English isn't that great, so he asks his British host, 'What ees theez "spcika yo wigt machina"?' His minder explains, so Pavarotti goes in.

When he comes out he asks another question: 'What is theez "no coach parties"?'

We don't make jokes like that about fat oil companies.

But, I hear you thinking, all that corporate corpulence was okay back in the middle of the twentieth century. It doesn't work now. No? What about Bill Gates? The world's richest nerd has modelled his Microsoft Empire on the oil business. His organisation has absorbed not only every branch of the PC business, but has made it almost impossible for any competitor to get any product into operating systems. Go into PC World – every box on every shelf has the word 'Microsoft' on it somewhere. He is the new Standard Oil. And to prove it, the US government has taken legal action against him under the self-same anti-trust laws that were used to try and break up the mighty oil-company monopolies of the last century. Just about the only competition that Gates has is in the form of Apple Mac, with their far superior operating system, but he has effectively gluttoned them out to a small, specialist sector of the market.

Gluttonous businesses stop little businesses getting in.

T H E   S I N   O F   G L U T T O N Y   –   M I C R O S O F T

It barely needs any explanation. Microsoft is the modern-day embodiment of corporate greed. From a nothing to a global giant in little more than 20 years, and now a virtually inescapable part of the computer landscape. Gate's goliath, notwithstanding the outcome of hugely complex legal proceedings in the United States, has built its epic success on embedding itself into every aspect of business and personal computing process.

The Windows operating system is virtually ubiquitous and the Office software package is the starting point for most people's computing consciousness. But not content with domination in those markets, Microsoft has extended its reach into some areas of hardware and has recently emerged as the preeminent challenger to Sony in the gaming console arena.

It is Microsoft's gluttonous corporate style that has antagonised begrudging users, competitors, and, most significantly the US authorities. It has made Bill Gates one of the richest men in the world, put Seattle on the business map, and secured Microsoft's position as the first truly global software brand.

When Luciano Pavarotti sits in a cinema seat, those either side will always be empty.

That is the power of corporate gluttony.

When Rupert Murdoch, the Global Glutton-in-Chief, sits his corporate backside in a seat, the next two countries go empty. Murdoch prides himself as a man of values. He is undoubtedly, by inclination, politically of the right. While his biggest selling British 'red top' newspaper, the *Sun*, unstintingly supported Margaret Thatcher throughout her reign, he referred to Lenin as 'the great teacher' and while a student at Oxford it is said that he even had a bust of the great Communist leader on the mantle in his room.

Good gluttons know how to pick the choicest cuts from any table.

Even though he has always been a staunch Conservative (and through the 1980s many of the pages of his newspapers looked as if they had been photocopied straight out of the Conservative Party Manifesto), when he was a student at Oxford Murdoch ran for office in the Labour club. This wasn't because he had assumed some sort of left-wing student radicalism, but simply that he couldn't survive without his greed for power. In fact, he was disqualified after distributing flyers for breaking rules that prohibit self-promotion – a practice that was to come back to him in spades as a newspaper magnate.

He breaks the rules of gentlemanly conduct, he metaphorically pigs out and he's made a career out of doing just that ever since.

When Rupert Murdoch, the Global Glutton-in-Chief, sits his corporate backside in a seat, the next two countries go empty.

In *The Australian*, the newspaper that Murdoch founded, he wanted a serious quality paper to give him credibility and political influence. In 1972 he supported Labour Party candidate Gough Whitlam as Prime Minister of Australia. Not content to have supported the successful candidate, and with that to enjoy the benefits of a friendly administration, his gluttony spurred him to ask the Australian PM to make him ambassador to London. His request was denied.

Still smarting from not getting his own way, in 1975, instead of supporting Whitlam, Murdoch supported the more conservative Malcolm Fraser and so did *The Australian*. He wasn't going to let little thing like principle get in the way of his gluttony.

'. . . nothing appeared in the paper if it didn't follow the line . . . most extraordinarily ruthless and one-sided   political coverage I think any of us can remember'. Mungo MacCullum, former political reporter The Australian.

Gluttons tend to be single-minded about their greed. Single-minded greed tends to lead to success.

Malcolm Fraser won and, following the election, papers were burned in the streets and journalists went on strike over Murdoch's ethical swings. But Murdoch already had his greedy mind's eye on a global television network. At his request a grateful Prime Minister, Malcolm Fraser, had Australian laws on foreign ownership of television stations changed, allowing Murdoch to maintain residency elsewhere, and to pursue his global feast.

The Carr family had owned the *News of the World*, the biggest selling newspaper in Britain, since 1891. When Robert Maxwell, himself a gluttonous corporate raider, threatened to buy the paper, the Carr family sought a white knight to save them. Rupert Murdoch described himself as that white knight, promising the Carrs that he would not seek majority ownership. When the shareholders voted, they chose Murdoch over Maxwell because that was what the Carr family wanted, even though Maxwell was offering more money. Six months after the merger, Murdoch sought and gained majority control.

The *News of the World* is a weekly newspaper. Murdoch decided he also wanted a daily, so in 1969 he bought the *Sun*. He regarded journalism as a commodity to be consumed like any other. Under Murdoch, the prudish right-winger, the *Sun* started printing photos of topless models on page three. Even though he was a fully paid-up member of the union bashing club, Murdoch moulded the *Sun* in such a way that it was to be seen in the hands of every factory worker and shop steward in the land.

Even though he was a fully paid-up member of the union bashing club, Murdoch moulded the Sun in such a way that it was to be seen in the hands of every factory worker and shop steward in the land.

In the life of every business, one of three things will happen.
Either the company eventually dies.
Or it gets taken over by a competitor.
Or it takes over a competitor.

Gluttony is a life-support system for business.

In 1976 Murdoch bought the *New York Post*, the oldest continuously published daily in the United States. In 1981 Murdoch bought the 200-year-old *Times* of London. According to Andrew Neil, its former editor, because Murdoch already owned the *Sun* and the *News of the World*, his acquisition of the *Times* should have been referred to the monopolies commission, but it was not because Murdoch had the right political connections. No matter which hue those political connections need to be, Murdoch would always have the right ones.

Gluttons aren't fussy eaters.

The printing equipment at the *Times* was antiquated and the union refused to let the machines be updated for fear of losing jobs. Murdoch secretly began an operation to produce the newspapers with modern computer equipment. If he could produce the newspaper entirely independently of the union, he would take away any bargaining power the union had. Ten thousand former employees picketed in the streets surrounding the new operation, only to find themselves held back by barbed wire and a small army of officers from the Metropolitan Police force, supplied by Murdoch's friend the Home Secretary.

The Murdoch Empire has grown from its Australian base to cover huge areas of South Asia, North America and Europe. Newscorp and Fox in the United States, Datacom in Israel and Sky TV in Europe. If it's available in the world of broadcast media, the multi-billionaire Murdoch is a glutton for it – even if it means acquiring a new nationality. At various times he has been Australian, British and American.

Gluttony knows no national barriers.

The pattern has been a familiar one. Murdoch uses his ample financial girth as a battering ram to widen influence and market share and, together with political influence and the creation of satellite channels, his media regime is all-powerful. No government has ever stood up to Murdoch. Now he has even become an ally of the object of the *Sun* newspaper's ridicule for so many years – the British Labour Party.

Has Murdoch really changed his party political allegiance towards Labour?

The more realistic answer is that the Labour party has changed its political stance towards Murdoch, the very man who put countless union members out of work with the help of Margaret Thatcher's police force.

That is success thanks to gluttony in action.

The Ten Commandments
of committing the sin of

GLUTTONY

---

1 Enough is never enough.

Peter Bazalgette is a highly successful British television producer. He started out by helping to create a highly successful programme called *Food and Drink*, at which point most of us might reasonably move on to other projects. Not Bazalgette. He added a competition element to *Food and Drink* and made it *Ready Steady Cook*. He swapped food for wallpaper and made *Ready Steady Cook* into *Changing Rooms*, then he swapped rooms for gardens and came up with *Ground Force*. Then he combined the two into *When Changing Rooms Met Ground Force*.

Run down the television listings this week. The schedules are splattered with food, DIY and gardening shows. Most of them are exactly the same as each other. Most of these are from Bazalgette, and he still keeps going. Having joined forces with Endemol, he brought us *Big Brother* . . . then *Celebrity Big Brother* . . . then *Big Brother II*, while every other television producer in the land is looking to come up with virtually the same format.

2 Observe everything.

Okay, so you are unlikely to be the next umbrella handle magnate, armed with a knowledge of telegraph poles and Brussels sprouts. But what is the next opportunity? For example, do you play golf? What is the surface of a golf ball like? It's dimpled. Why? Because the indentations make the ball penetrate the air better. What else needs to penetrate the air? Cars? Planes? Two-hundred metre hurdlers? Could these use dimples? Probably not, but dismissing ideas no matter how fanciful never got anyone a nice new house. What else around you has an obscure purpose?

3 Question everything.

The Romans occasionally used to notice animals chewing the bark of certain trees. Why did dumb animals do that? Were they hungry? No, there was plenty of proper food about. Were the animals stupid? Possibly, but all animals are pretty stupid and not all of them did it. The answer was that the animals felt ill. The bark contained a substance that made them feel better. It was aspirin. Creative books train us to ask 'What if?' Gluttons do it naturally.

4 Never tell anyone anything they don't need to know.

You've gone to the trouble of gaining this information. It's valuable. Don't give it away like the oil company messenger who missed out on a fortune. Don't shoot your mouth off in the wine bar about how you've got the next great money-spinner.

Coca Cola don't happily tell everyone else what their secret ingredient is.

5 There is nothing that isn't worth knowing.

Keep your ears open for anything and everything. Obviously I can't tell you what it is in particular you're looking for. Even if I could, I wouldn't. I follow my own sinning rules, as you'll discover when you read about the Sin of Avarice.

6 Even the best gluttons are short on time.

So learn to speed read. Skim the pages for key words. Pick up words and ideas you don't recognise. If you don't recognise them, then the chances are most other people haven't. Tuck away every piece of information you can. You will learn to retrieve those you need.

7 Ideas that aren't being used are wasted assets.

Good ideas are lying about in other people's heads like litter on the street waiting to be picked up. Ideas are worth more than material items. And if all else fails, it's easier to steal an idea than it is to steal a car.

8 From tiny acorns do mighty Sycamores grow.

One idea can lead to another, and another and another. Thomas Edison invented the phonograph in 1877. Two years later he invented the light bulb, then the moving picture camera, then the dictating machine and so on until he had amassed over 1000 patents on related inventions. Thomas Edison had no formal education. His introduction to inventing came when he was asked to devise a reliable printing machine. From that, everything else flowed. He absorbed all the knowledge he could and never stopped absorbing.

From Edison's ceaseless hunger for knowledge and patents, grew General Electric, which is still rarely ranked outside the top five largest corporations in the world.

9 Fiction is stranger than fact.

Movies, books, even occasionally, television shows are full of great ideas. Use them. The notable Austrian film director of the 1920s and 1930s, Fritz Lang, had one of his ideas borrowed to great effect by the American space programme of the 1960s. His 1926 movie, *Metropolis*, features a futuristic space launch. To heighten the tension of the scene, Lang devised the countdown.

There is no technical reason to count down backwards to a space launch, but when NASA needed to justify their huge expenditure on their space programme they decided to market it on network television. What they needed was excitement. The build-up to a space launch is pretty boring, so they stole Lang's 'countdown'. It made for great television, their audience were thrilled by it and their budget was secure. If one of them hadn't watched lots of old movies, NASA might never have got past their first rocket experiments.

10 Gluttony is a mental attitude.

Forget the nonsense about gluttony making you fat and lonely. That's just for overeaters of food. It's impossible to get fat bingeing on ideas.

Exercise on

GLUTTONY

Have you ever experienced something like this? You want to move house. Suddenly, everywhere you look there are 'for sale' signs; every other shop seems to be an estate agent. You overhear people in the office chatting about house prices and mortgage lenders. Are there really more signs and estate agents than there were yesterday? No, it's just that you have started to notice them, because you've started to focus on moving house.

Try this: look around you and notice all the things that are blue. Now look back at this page and try and remember all the things that were brown. Tricky? Probably. Your mind focuses on some things and deletes others – it simply can't focus on everything at once, so it filters what out what it doesn't think is useful.

What has this got to do with gluttony? Simple. If you know what you want, your mind will start focusing on it. Once your mind starts focusing, it's a short step to working out how to turn those goals into a reality.

To really live like a glutton, don't limit your goal setting to just one area of your life.

Have a go now. Write down some goals against each of these headings below.

Health & Energy ....

Relationships ....

Social ....

Financial ....

Career ....

Personal Development ....

How did that go? Did you stick to the headings? Did you stick to the space provided by each heading? Drongo! Does Pavarotti stick to the menu? Does Damien Hirst stick to the space provided? Gluttony is about richness, fullness, going for it with guns blazing.

Maybe this will help: imagine that it is many years hence. You are old and wrinkly and about to pop your clogs. You look back on your life and think, 'Bugger, if only I'd . . .' What do you wish you'd done? What do you regret not having, not achieving?

Do the exercise again, only this time use whatever categories are most useful to you. Get some blank paper or switch on the laptop and crank out the most gluttonous wish list of dreams, ambitions, goals and desires.

How did that go? A bit more gluttonous? Great . . .

Now rip that list up and start again. Be more outrageous, extravagant and ambitious. Pile your plate high, cram as much into your life as you can.

Now you have a juicy list. Read it through and savour it.

Put the list away and sleep on it. Get the list out again tomorrow. Tomorrow is the time to start prioritising and planning. We tend to overestimate what we can achieve in a week or a month, but dramatically underestimate what we can achieve in five years or ten. You don't want to be Mr Creosote, you do want a longer, fuller, gluttonous life.

The Sin of

LUST

'The expense of spirit in a waste of shame is lust in action: and till action, lust is perjured, murderous, bloody, full of blame, Savage, extreme rude, not to trust; Enjoyed no sooner but despised straight.'

William Shakespeare

'I take it I'm not getting the complete works tonight, then?'

Anne Hathaway

I
T IS NOT DIFFICULT TO UNDERSTAND WHY THE BIBLE should be so hung up on the Sin of Lust. Lust is seen as a selfish little sin. It is about self-gratification with no regard for anyone else. Lust goes to sleep before breakfast, hides dormant and furtive only to reawaken towards closing time. Lust is lechery, lewdness, salaciousness and wantonness. Lust is an endless list of similes for industrial-strength randiness. Lust, in the eyes of religion, is pure, no nonsense, let's just get on with it and never mind what your name is, I just want it and so do you. Sex.

The religious interpretation of lust is, in short, the carnal cravings of the body, or, more specifically, the bits of the body usually tucked away in the trousers. Nice religions, like nice girls and aged maiden aunts, don't enjoy talking about those bits and don't want anyone else talking about them either. Lust is represented by religion as the manifestation of a dirty mind. But the very creation of the Sin of Lust is itself a manifestation of lust.

Take this example. A young Catholic lad of about fourteen goes to see the local priest to ask him a question.

'Father,' says the lad, 'what does the word 'vice' mean?'

The priest replies that vice is a corrupting influence on society, the sinful activities of filthy degenerates who commit depraved acts; fallen women who debase themselves for the sexual gratification of adulterous husbands. Vice is the purest wickedness of those who perpetrate the most disgusting and foul acts of venality. And then the priest asks: 'Why do you, a young boy of only fourteen ask me that?'

The lad replies, 'The school has just made me vice-captain of the cricket team.'

Generations of priests have preached that the Sin of Lust will have our dangly bits roasting in Hell for all eternity, and, of course, for thousands of years they could point quite convincingly to some pretty nasty sexually transmitted diseases as evidence. This is probably why the Catholic Church still makes such a fuss about the use of condoms. If you can enjoy a bit of good, old-fashioned, lustful rumpy-pumpy without fear of contracting a dose of the clap, then this theory about Satan applying a burning hornet's nest to your pubic region starts to look a bit shaky. If only Durex had been around in the sixteenth century, Henry VIII, the supreme head of the Church of the England no less, might not have been sent to his grave by a nasty case of galloping gonorrhoea.

Generations of priests have preached that the Sin of Lust will have our dangly bits roasting in Hell for all eternity

The Church's anti-lust campaign hasn't stopped a fair proportion of priests putting countless buns in the ovens of good Catholic girls, or trying to slip a healing hand up the cassocks of generations of unsuspecting choirboys. Are these hypocritical acts so very different from those of successful businesses? How many profitable organisations preach the free market, but do their very best to destroy it in the cause of satisfying their lust?

Jeffrey Archer is a human dynamo of lust-fired energy. He has been phenomenally successful despite the small handicap of being immeasurably close to talentless. He is also currently incarcerated in one of Her Majesty's Prisons, but that's another story. Archer, the son of a womanising fraudster (believe it or not) and father of a fraudulent city trader, has built his entire life on lust. As a young man, he lusted after the public success he saw enjoyed by fine athletes, so he had a British Olympic Team blazer knocked up at the tailors and made himself a sporting hero. He lusted after a socially and intellectually superior wife, the fragrant Mary, so he got himself into Oxford with just three 'O' levels (and a degree from an American university that doesn't exist). He lusted after the kind of power he saw politicians using to exercise their will on the nation, so he became the youngest ever British MP, except of course for the four others who were younger than him. When he lusted after the smart suits he saw his rivals wearing, he walked out of an upmarket store with three over his arm (suits, not rivals). When he fell from grace, Archer still lusted after cash and success, the type enjoyed by writers of the blockbuster paperbacks he saw at airports, and so he became a best-selling novelist. He managed this, if the rumours are to be believed, without ever actually writing a best-selling word of his own.

He lusted after the millionaire lifestyle, so he became a millionaire.

There are men who need only to brush against a female on a crowded bus to suddenly have the ineluctable need to satisfy their lust. Archer is apparently someone who needs only to be in the same postcode area as a woman to have an urgent need to rush off to the nearest brothel.

Lord Archer of Weston Super Mare is the perfect example of a lust triumphing over talent. Lust will propel him back.

Jeffrey Archer is apparently someone who needs only to be in the same postcode area as a woman to have an urgent need to rush off to the nearest brothel.

It's better to have lust and lost than never to have lust at all.

Although it is remarkably easy to make money out of other people's lust – Hugh Hefner didn't get a private Playboy Boeing 707 selling Bibles on street corners – I don't want to leave you with the impression that I've swallowed a double dose of Pfizer's finest. Let me assure you that the Sin of Lust doesn't have its eyes fixed exclusively on the groin. My aim isn't to develop a generation of porn-producing smut barons. The *Sin to Win* bible has a slightly different definition for lust; it's the need of gratification.

Setting long-term goals is all well and good. Armed with the Sin of Pride, you will know with absolute confidence that you will achieve whatever objectives you set yourself. Why? Because you believe in yourself. But, as a realist, you'll understand that ticking off goals on your list can take time. Lust allows you to break large goals into bite-sized challenges and gives you a reward every time you do so.

On a rare visit to a religious bookshop, I bought something called *The Workshop on the Seven Deadly Sins*. What a bundle of laughs that book gave me. It is little wonder that we characterise Born-Again Christians as dullards, lacking excitement and hedonism.

The book tells the tale of a nineteen-year-old German youth born in an era before the fall of Communism. Apparently this plucky teenager, not content with joyriding in a Skoda, flew a single-engine Cessna hundreds of miles over Russian territory, completely undetected, and landed in the middle of Red Square. Not surprisingly, to save face, the Russian Government interrogated and arrested him, before letting him go free.

To you or I, this might simply be a story of lust: no thought for the consequences, no consideration of what may lie ahead, just the thrill of a challenge. Hedonism. Living a full and exciting life.

To the authors of *The Workshop*, the plucky kid might well have shaken hands, exchanged phone-numbers, gone out on a few dates and slept with the Devil himself.

Lust is the essence of immediate self-gratification. It's about doing the unimaginable. It's about grabbing whatever you can, as soon as you can. It is recognising that situations can change in a heartbeat. Why should doing something that is pleasurable as soon as possible be considered a bad thing? Why should doing something that is profitable as soon as possible be considered a bad thing? Why should doing anything sooner rather later be a bad thing?

S A I N T   O R   S I N N E R ?

Donatien Alphonse François de Sade (1740–1814) – or the Marquis to his friends – is remembered not only as the father of sadism but by some critics as the freest spirit who ever lived. He lived a life full of orgies – from 1773 to 1777 he had hired a harem of young girls as sexual slaves – and argued for torture and sodomy in his infamous novels *Les 120 Journées De Sodome* and *Justine*. Sure, he spent some time in prison but, unlike most of the French aristiocracy, he survived the Revolution and made it to the ripe old age of 74, enjoying more than his fair share of rough and tumble along the way.

'Less haste, more speed' may be a fine motto for the amphetamine production business, but when does it do any good anywhere else?

Self-gratification can be channelled in various directions. It may be the cravings for simple pleasures of the body, such as fine foods or wines, or it can be for pleasures of the mind or eye; going to the ballet is a form of lust.

What's so wicked about setting goals?
What's so evil about wanting to make yourself happy?
What's so immoral about craving new experiences?

Set goals. Make yourself happy.
Crave new experiences.
Live for the moment.

There is no doubt that good, old-fashioned sexual lust can be converted into a profit. As a student, I worked one summer vacation in a seaside pub serving beer, bottling up and generally acting as the handyman. One of my duties every Friday morning was to empty the condom machine. Not to take the money out, that was the landlord's job, but to take the condoms out. Every Friday night, countless alcohol-induced lust-enticed young men who thought they might be in for a night of passion with the top-heavy barmaid, would put their hard-earned cash into the condom machine. Naturally, no condoms ever appeared. And how many customers ever complained or asked for their money back? In the seven weeks I was there, not one. As a contingency, in case anyone did ever complain, the landlord would make some apology about the terrible service you get from vending machine companies and simply hand over a packet of three from his emergency personal stock.

On Mondays, I replaced all but half-a-dozen packets of condoms in the machine, plus six quid, and the vending machine man arrived on Tuesdays. Now, even habitual drunks aren't likely to fall for that scam more than once or twice, but as it was the seaside, there was a fresh set of punters every week. The pure profit over a good weekend was in excess of £300 for less than five minutes' work.

That landlord used the blind lust in others to his self-advantage. He remembered the lust he had felt at that age, and used that knowledge for quick portion of financial self-gratification every weekend.

It does seem to be true that most people who have an insatiable lust for success in business, sport or the arts also seem to have a pretty high libido to match. Grand Prix motor racing is a prime example. The old cliché about fast cars being penis

THE SIN OF LUST – EASYEVERYTHING

The greatest entrepreneurs are always lustful. When they see an opportunity they react immediately, uninhibited by the sort of conservatism and conspicuously sane thinking that most established businesses have to deal with. Stelios Haji-Ioannou, the heir of a Greek shipping dynasty, is an entrepreneur *par excellence*. He started his budget airline, easyJet, in 1995, spotting a demand for a no-frills carrier to a narrow range of business and holiday destinations.

The easyGroup has now expanded into car rental (easyRentacar) and Internet cafes (easyEverything). Stelios has built the brand around his own ebullient and easy-going persona, featuring in its television adverts and popping up all over the media whenever he gets the chance to promote his strongly pro-consumer philosophy. It's all about making things easy for consumers, both operationally and fiscally.

His next move looks set to be into financial services under the moniker easyMoney – a credit card that offers an unprecedented amount of flexibility to its users. Stelios' lustful approach to business makes it virtually impossible to predict where his easy empire will extend to next, but it also underpins his success – he is completely unintimidated about taking on the big boys.

substitutes seems to have a pretty high truth content, although if cars really were penis substitutes, rather than drive fast around the roads, we'd surely be reversing them in and out of the garage all day. Most of today's Grand Prix drivers are seen in the pits with a different model on their arms at each race. The sexual conquests of the likes of Eddie Irvine are legendary, although it is no coincidence that the notches on his headboard were more in danger of causing the bed to collapse when he was winning races for Ferrari than when he's failing to finish races for Jaguar. Even David Coulthard, who would have trouble winning a beauty contest on a dark night during a power cut, goes through fiancées faster than he does the start/finish line. One former Grand Prix star of the 1970s even admitted to getting such a thrill out of leading races that he frequently got an erection in the car. He was the one who could change gear without taking a hand off the steering wheel.

In part, this excess of sexual appetite can be put down to the drivers' young age range and fitness regime, which puts them in a superhuman state of physical prowess. Most top athletes are similar, although many have had their libidos severely dented by taking the wrong hormones. Russian teenage girls didn't need to go out looking for boys when they could stay at home and watch their own penis grow.

Russian teenage girls didn't need to go out looking for boys when they could stay at home and watch their own penis grow.

It is quite difficult to disassociate lust from sexual desire. There is no doubt that lust for virtually anything is driven in the same way as sex. Food is a classic example. The desire for chocolate has been proven scientifically to be exactly the same chemical desire as the desire for sex. Anyone who develops the habit of eating extremely hot Indian food, stuffed full of the hottest chillies, becomes addicted to the same chemical that hits the brain during the moment of orgasm. Likewise, the desire for real financial success – not merely enough money to be comfortable on but skip-loads of cash that could wallpaper a small palace in twenties – is a desire driven by one of the same group of sexually driven chemicals. This should come as no surprise. Sex is the very foundation stone of the survival of the human race. And lust is what makes the human race go after sex, food and everything else, that has been piled on the wish list as survival has been succeeded by civilisation and society. Lust is what made man climb down out of the trees to pursue his quarry, whether it was fresh meat or a fresh female of the species. Just try having a bit of nookie in an old oak tree and see how well you get on. And that's after you've been bored with surviving on a diet of birds' nests. With the possible exception of Swampy, the anti-road campaigner, no one can have sex in a tree.

Lust cares only for the pursuit of a challenge
and its inevitable conquest.

A better way to think of lust as a goal-getting facilitator is through the creed of hedonism. This is neat little doctrine, which believes the pursuit of pleasure is not only the highest good but also a matter of principle. The hedonists even developed the notion that moral values can be defined in terms of material and sensual pleasures. Religious orders frown on this sort of talk as a form of heresy. If you embrace hedonism, you embrace materialism and to be called 'materialist' is to be accused of being shallow. Why? The desire for money and possessions is seen by the Church as being in conflict with their teachings on several levels. They say you can't possibly have a desire for wealth if you also have spiritual values. The ultimate conclusion of the materialist is that there is nothing in their existence over and above physical matter. And the natural conclusion to be drawn from that theory is: there are no gods.

There is only one thing wrong with this branch of religious indoctrination. It makes as much sense as David Icke on – or off – acid.

SAINT OR SINNER?

A news story from Colombia recently told of some ingenious thieves. Police had uncovered the *modus operandi* of a group of prostitutes who would stand on the roadside in Bogota and offer their naked breasts for men to lick. But hapless punters who took advantage of this lusty offer would find themselves feeling very sleepy. The women had drugged their breats so they could steal from the unwarey suckers.

The Church was founded on subjugating the poor and ignorant. If the poor and ignorant acquire wealth, they might be able to afford to get themselves educated and churches would start to look a bit thin 'bums on pew-wise'. In fact, if a religion

THE SIN OF LUST — TINY ROWLAND

The London and Rhodesia Company was incorporated in 1909 but it wasn't until the mid-1960s that it began to assume the shape for which it eventually became famous. That was under the control of its legendarily lustful chief executive Tiny Rowland, an utterly irrepressible man determined to be stopped by nothing.

Conservative Prime Minister Edward Heath was so distressed by Rowland's aggressive style that he famously dubbed him 'the unacceptable face of capitalism'.

His success in Africa was based on the speed and skill with which he made friends with some of the region's most important leaders. He reputedly bribed newly elected government officials to secure access to precious mineral resources, an accusation that he certainly never denied during his lifetime.

He managed, for example, to make money out of Mozambique during the 1980s, when no one else would have dreamed of getting involved somewhere so unstable politically. The secret — he used his own mercenaries to protect his enormous cotton interests.

Rowland turned the company into a major business. In 1989, at its peak, it reported profits of £272 million, compared with just £158,000 in 1961. During the 1970s, more than 80% of its profits came from Africa. Lonrho, his holding company, had thousands of subsidiaries including the *Observer* newspaper.

His success was underpinned, not just by a preparedness to use tactics that others wouldn't dream of employing, but by a ruthlessness and impetuosity. He was lustful *par excellence.*

is worth having, why isn't it worth having for a rich man? Why can't a wealthy, happy person have spiritual needs? He can, but it doesn't suit the Church. If you are a conscientious congregation member, as soon as you acquire a few bob, you'll find that the vicar wants a handout for the organ restoration fund. That's why the Christian Bible says it's 'easier for a camel to pass through the eye of a needle than for a rich man to enter the Kingdom of God'.

Well, if you are a rich a man, there's a simple fix for pushing that camel through the eye of a needle. Get yourself a very big needle made.

The Church may not like this lustful hedonism thing, but it was lust that led Alexander the Great to rule the known civilised world before the age of twenty-six. It was hedonism that sent the Portuguese to sail round Africa to the Far East in search of silks and spices. It was lust that sent Christopher Columbus in search of the faster sea route only to find that the United States was in the way. It was hedonistic lust that led Napoleon to create the first European Union. It was lust for a better, wealthier, life that sent Europeans ever further west across what is now the United States of America and it was lust that sent American men to the moon. Yet

SAINT OR SINNER?

Hugh Heffner – say no more. It is difficult to think of a man who is as envied by the male population of the world as Hugh Hefner. Not only is Hef unbelievably wealthy, the owner of mansions inhabited by centrefolds and a soft porn empire second to none, all created from his vision of a magazine which catered to the tastes and desires of the average guy, but he plans to spend the rest of his days with seven large-breasted blonde girls. 'Picasso had his blue period. I am in my blonde period.' claims the aging Lothario.

again it was man with a healthy lust for life as well as for sex who decided they would go – John F. Kennedy. Lust that results in a 25,000 mph trip to the moon and regular sex romps with Marilyn Monroe can't be all bad.

Lust that results in a 25,000 mph trip to the moon and regular sex romps with Marilyn Monroe can't be all bad.

Lust teaches us to live life to the full.
To do that we need to take risks.
Sometimes we succeed. Sometimes we fail.

Failure, to a man who embraces lust, encourages him
to take another risk. Eventually he will succeed.

The lesson? Failure is only temporary.

Quite perversely, if it hadn't been for that most obscene act of naked aggressive lust of the twentieth century, the First World War, America's lust to possess the moon might have taken quite a lot longer. During 1919, in between the cease-fire and the signing of a peace treaty, the once mighty German battle fleet languished at anchor in captivity under the watchful eyes of the British in Scapa Flo in the Orkney Islands. As the Germans were prisoners of war, they were only allowed newspapers that were at least a week old, lest they got themselves up to speed with political events back home and decided to join in any restarted conflict. In fact, the fleet was in no fit state to fight, but when it appeared that the German government would refuse to sign the papers accepting total, humiliating defeat, it seemed that the First

World War – Part Two would be starting any day. Scapa Flow is a place with which most Americans are not familiar, yet it played a crucial role in getting their men to the moon.

In November 1918, under the terms of the Armistice ending hostilities of The Great War, Germany agreed to let her powerful navy be guarded by the allies. A total of 74 ships were called upon to be voluntarily interned. These vessels were constructed of the best steel available. This once proud navy, which had been intended to gratify the Kaiser's lust for total sea power, was now disarmed, manned only by skeleton crews. Seven months dragged on, and the Peace Treaty negotiations seemed to be deadlocked. Britain and her allies threatened to resume hostilities if the Germans did not sign on the dotted line.

THE SIN OF LUST – PAUL RAYMOND

Paul Raymond has built one of the UK's most successful pornography businesses with a long list of some of the best-selling top-shelf magazines. That in itself gives him a strong claim to having built an empire on lust. It made £23 million profit in 2000 on sales of 41 million – not bad. The pornography business globally – pure lust – is gigantically profitable and one of the few industries to have found a means of making a mint out of the Internet.

However, it is Raymond's property portfolio that has propelled him up into the ranks of the mega-rich. And that too was assembled through lust. Raymond long ago seized the opportunity to buy up cheap and run-down property in the then unfashionable and dingy Soho district of central London. Now it is worth millions and he can sit back and enjoy giant rental returns. The *Sunday Times* rich list in 2001 estimated Raymond's worth at about £650 million, of which his property assets were reckoned to be worth about half.

Admiral Reuter, the German officer in charge of the interned Fleet, decided to order the sinking of his ships rather than have them fall into the hands of the British. What he didn't know was that the German government had fallen two days after he read the latest out-of-date newspaper he had been allowed, and that an armistice, putting a final seal on peace, was to be signed later that week. On 21 June 1919, after the Royal Navy left Scapa Flo for exercises, he gave the order to scuttle the entire Imperial German High Seas Fleet.

Since the Second World War, when the testing of atomic weapons began, every particle of air on our planet has been contaminated with nuclear radiation. Not hugely, but nonetheless it is everywhere. The production of high-grade stainless steel involves the ingestion of massive quantities of air, to the extent that all modern production is slightly radioactive. Try running a Geiger counter over your cutlery tray. In order to function accurately, an atomic clock has to be cased in completely radiation-free steel. In order to navigate accurately all the way to the moon, Neil, Buzz and the one whose name no one can ever remember, had to use atomic clocks. To get the steel, NASA pillaged the remains of the German Battle fleet at Scapa Flo.

What kind of undying lust does it take to come up with that kind of resourcefulness? The kind of lust that is satisfied by firing the most powerful rockets faster than any other human-built object has ever travelled. And if firing huge penis-shaped objects straight up as fast as possible isn't penis substitution – then nothing is.

When was the last time you took a chance?
When was the last time you grabbed an opportunity?
When was the last time you threw caution to the wind?

**What great stories about your life are you
going to tell your grandkids?**

The only difference between plant life and animal life is lust.
Conversely, a lack of lust equates to a lack of vision.

We all have lust. Lust is entirely natural. The only difference between plant life and animal life is lust. They both have sex, they both breath and eat and drink, but plants don't have enough lust for them to get about and do something about their desires, they have to wait virtually motionless for a keen gardener to do it all for them. A gardener is nothing more than an animal that has developed a better lust for life and preferably, a better lust for horticulture.

Conversely, a lack of lust equates to a lack of vision.

In the mid-1870s a Scottish scientist working as professor of vocal physiology at Boston University started to experiment with devices that might help the hard of hearing. He soon came up with a contraption, which he called the 'hearing aid'. It was an ungainly device, consisting of a huge earpiece connected by wires to a rudimentary carbon-filled microphone. When he tried it out, the professor and his assistant both took the roles of deaf people, each having a hearing aid attached to their heads and microphone in front of their mouths. It took a lab assistant to point out that what this professor, one Alexander Graham Bell, had actually invented was the telephone. Having filed his patent, Bell's lust was aroused and he went on to found one of the United States' most successful communications empires.

As an aside, it is often assumed that telephones 'ring' because a man named Bell invented them. If only he'd been called Drake – to this day – we'd all be saying 'Bye now, I'll give you a quack tomorrow.'

When Bell came to demonstrate his first commercially available telephone before an audience of businessmen and politicians, a senior official from the White House Cabinet was so impressed that he said: 'I can imagine a time when there will be one of these machines in every major city in America.' No lust there, then. Perhaps he was relative of C.P. Scott, the noted editor of the *Manchester Guardian*, who wrote of a similarly ground-breaking invention: 'Television – the word is half Latin and half Greek. No good will come of this device.'

Alexander Fleming was famously a great pioneering scientist. But after he published details of his discovery of penicillin in 1920, it was a full ten years before he or anyone else bothered to put it into commercial production. Can you imagine how much Pfizer would have lost if they'd hung about for decade after accidentally discovering Viagra?

Pfizer knows a thing or two about how to exploit lust when they see it.

Some years ago, in the closing stages of the Vietnam war, the Washington correspondent of the London *Times* rang round all the embassies asking what they were most hoping for that Christmas. The Russian Ambassador said he hoped for peace in the world and an end to the conflict in South-East Asia. The French Ambassador replied that he wanted the UN to increase their famine aid programme to Africa, while the British Ambassador said he wanted a box of chocolates and a bottle of whisky.

We all have natural, in-built lust, to one extent or another. It's how we use it that makes the difference.

The Ten Commandments
of committing the sin of

LUST

1 Let lust make you passionate.

Richard Branson has amassed a personal fortune valued at anything from £750 million upwards. He started out by selling LPs by mail-order from a telephone box. When Virgin Records was at its most successful, he sold it. He introduced Space Invader machines to pubs. When bars had more varieties of electronic games machines than beers, he sold out.   Richard Branson has no lust for money, but he does have a passion for business and the power that goes with it. He is also one of those sexually charged, lust-motivated types. Just take a look at the stewardesses on his airline compared to those on others and guess why he attends as many new trolley-dolly induction courses as he possibly can. For someone who appears to be a financial octopus, his passion makes him remarkably single-minded. He will spend months negotiating a deal, and then apparently suddenly lose interest and drop it like a hot brick. As with sexual, lusty passion, if better fulfilment can be seen elsewhere, that's where he'll be.

2 Lust is desire.

Most people desire wealth. Sure, there are those who say that if they win the lottery, they'd still go to work and so on. In which case, if they really don't want to win anything they should enter the Readers Digest Prize Draw. There was a classic scam, which was more or less legal, in Ireland during the 1960s. (It probably also happened in the 1950 and the 1940s, but it worked every time.) Two regular punters who both lusted after wealth, but could think only of betting on horses as a way to find it, realised that, for poor people, betting is a mug's game. So they became tipsters. They tipped the winning horses, two races in a row, for free and then asked their happy customers for a large down payment for the third tip. They got upwards of a thousand pounds each out of 150 punters for one tip. The horse didn't win, but they did. They already had their money.

3 Lust leads to answers.

How did the Irish tipsters correctly predict the winners of the first two races? Easy. They sent tips out only on four-horse races, tipping every horse in the race. When they knew the result, they sent their next set of tips only to those punters who had been sent the winner. They did it again, just to convince any doubting Thomases, and then struck for gold. Their only investment was a pile of envelopes, a copy of the *Sporting Life* and some postage stamps. They got the money for that by staying out of the betting shop for month.

4 Lust is challenge.

A business acquaintance of mine was one of those who benefited hugely from the lust-fuelled money frenzy of the late 1980s. Houses that were worth £50,000 at the most were changing hands for a quarter of a million. Cars that cost £20,000 on the forecourt could be driven round the corner and sold for double that. He recognised that this was lust being channelled incorrectly and set himself a challenge – how to make a load of money, when everyone else was almost certain to lose theirs any day now. In 1989, he owned a small house in the country. It wasn't a grand house but he found that it was valued at £240,000. He realised that this was stupid; a two-bedroom cottage couldn't possibly be worth that. It was more or less a starter home, for goodness sake.

So he sold it. He got £245,000 because the buyer was so desperate to jump on the bandwagon that he offered a five grand sweetener for a quick deal. Nine months later, my friend bought an exactly similar house in the same area for £70,000.

5 Lust sells.

Although advertising and promotion work largely on envy, in the case of red-bloodied males, a bit of lust thrown in never does any harm. Even in this politically correct age, cars at motor shows have scantily clad young women with unfeasibly perfect bodies draped all over them. And it's no coincidence that no man in a television car ad has ever had an ugly girlfriend. Come Christmas or birthdays, diligent boyfriends make beelines for the prettiest girl on the perfume counter. In working-class areas, where men always buy the drinks, canny landlords will only ever employ female staff. It's quite simple: use good-looking women in any context whatsoever, so long as you're selling to men, or lesbians.

6 Let Lust satisfy your craving.

In 1994, Michael Schumacher had yet to win a world drivers' championship. At the final race of the season, only one man could beat him – Damon Hill, who arguably had the better car. Schumacher didn't win the race, didn't even finish it, but he won the world championship and has taken two more since. He is undoubtedly regarded as the best driver of the age, possibly of any age, and yet his lust for championship glory led him to cheat. Legally cheat, but cheat nonetheless. As the race began to unfold, Schumacher quickly established a lead over his rival, but in his enthusiasm to win, he overcooked a corner and crashed, damaging his suspension. The car was still just about mobile, but certainly in no condition to finish the race.

As Hill bore down on Schumacher's stricken car, sure to take the lead and possibly the title, the German knew exactly what to do without giving it a second thought. Hill had to score points to take the championship. If Hill didn't finish, Schumacher was champion. So he drove his stricken car back out on to the track in to the path of the unsighted Hill, whose own car was irreparably damaged. Schumacher won his first world title sitting in a broken car by the side of the road a good hour before the end of the race.

7 Use your lust. Don't let your lust use you.

Spool forward a few years. Schumacher has the chance to take his third title and the first for Ferrari since the 1970s. His passion is still there. The situation is the same as with Hill a few years before, but this time Schumacher's rival is the Canadian Jacques Villeneuve.

Schumacher is again in the lead, but his car's handling is beginning to deteriorate. Villeneuve, one of the best over-takers in the business, makes a dive for the inside, the corner is his and possibly the race and the championship too. This time, Schumacher didn't have the excuse of deranged steering, so he simply wrenched the wheel to the right and bounced into the side of Villeneuve's car. His lust for the title had overtaken him at the same time as did Villeneuve.

Unfortunately for the German ace, Villeneuve's car was in such a position as not to be badly harmed. He went on to gain the championship. Schumacher damaged his own car, forcing him to retire from the race and watch his rival win. He also damaged his reputation. This time, deliberate action was filmed in full colour by the camera mounted above his head. He was thrown out of that year's results. A salutatory tale of letting lust rule.

Like he gives a monkey's.

8 Lust is optimism.

I recently visited San Francisco. It was a busy period in the city, being a carnival weekend, and I couldn't be too fussy about accommodation arrangements. In the event, I found myself in a delightful French-style, *fin de siècle* hotel, sadly in the only really rough district of the city. San Francisco, being the city of peace and goodwill, has recently bulldozed all of its cheaply available apartment blocks and has a terrible homeless problem. One evening, as I walked up towards Union Square, I found myself confronted by a terrifying sight.

He was about seven feet tall, with an eight-foot beard and matted hair to match. He was filthy, to the point that his once white skin looked as if it had been prepared to make a pair of black suede shoes. He wore little but a tattered blanket that flea-ridden lice would have rejected as unsanitary. He approached me, breaking away from a similar group of down and outs, happily cooking crack over a burning car, and said: 'Excuse me, sir. Could you help me out of fix? I urgently need to raise 75 cents to buy a copy of the *Wall Street Journal*.'

His lust for life, which gives optimism at the most unlikely times, was still there.

9 Lust can work for you even if you don't know it.

There was an attractive but rather overweight woman who worked in the London office of a large firm of accountants. She became infatuated with one of the partners, who was available but showed no interest in her.

She decided that her bulging tummy and fleshy thighs were the problem and so went on a fitness and healthy diet regime. After eight months she was down to a trim size eight and looking great. The senior partner still showed no interest. So, deciding her lowly position in the firm might be the problem, she worked at promotion, gained qualifications and improved her status. Still nothing. So she thought that perhaps, as he had never shown any interest in women at the practice, the object of her desire didn't approve of office romances. She got a better job elsewhere, at which time her quarry did at last invite her out to dinner. They discussed business deals between their two companies, but little else. So she kept going. Kept improving in search of satisfying her lust.

She was running her own multi-national specialist accounting firm before she found the guy was gay. But look how successful her desire had made her meanwhile.

10 A lust for life is a lust for success.

Lust is not there to be suppressed by the teachings of your priest, the late Mary Whitehouse, or the British Board of Film Censors. It's there to be enjoyed.

Exercise on

LUST

When you made a list of goals for gluttony, did you put anything in for today or this week? To flex your lust muscles, make a list of ten things you could do in the next half an hour that would bring you pleasure and satisfaction. Choose at least one and do it.

If you're struggling to think of ten, read this through and then close your eyes and imagine it. Imagine you are holding half of a big juicy lemon. See its shiny yellow skin and the juice dribbling out of it. Bring the lemon closer to your mouth. Imagine the lemony smell, feel the waxy lemon skin in your hand. Now imagine that you are bringing the lemon closer and closer to your mouth and take a nice big bite out of it.

Close your eyes and try it now.

What happened? Chances are your mouth filled with saliva, just as if you had been eating a real lemon. I'm not suggesting that lust is about getting into the *Guinness Book of Records* for lemon eating, the interesting thing to note is the following.

The nervous system does not know the difference between a real and a vividly imagined event.

If you want immediate gratification, but you're having a bad-hair day, take an imaginary holiday. Your mind won't know the difference and you'll instantly chill out and enjoy the moment. Men have some natural skills in this area. Some lusty statistician worked out that blokes think about sex hundreds of times a day.

The sad thing is there are usually loads of times when we could enjoy ourselves and we simply don't grasp the opportunity because we are being miserable gits. Remember that scale of 1 to 10 where 1 is feeling lousy and 10 is feeling great? It's our choice where we play from; it's our choice how we react to events.

Have a look at these letters 'opportunityisnowhere'.

What did you read? 'Opportunity is nowhere'? Or 'opportunity is now here'? Lust is very definitely about seeing and seizing the opportunity now here.

Have you ever heard someone say 'I can laugh now, but at the time it was awful'? Why not laugh now? Why bother to wait? I once went on a package holiday and the flight back was delayed by twelve hours. Most of the passengers went ballistic. They started f-ing and blinding at the reps – all their relaxation from two weeks in the sun evaporated in an instant. Then I overheard one guy say to his mate: 'Fantastic, a legitimate excuse to skive work tomorrow – and I reckon that rep with the long blond hair will soon be in need of my, err, "TLC" after putting up with all that abuse.'

The lusty ones will always find the silver lining in any cloud.

Next time you feel peeved off about a situation try this. Ask yourself:

◆ What's funny about this?
◆ What's good about this?

The first time you try, your automatic response might be unprintable and pretty negative, but if you persevere, you'll start to see the 'opportunity now here'.

The Sin of

ANGER

'The man who gets angry at the right things and with the right people and in the right way and at the right time and for the right length of time, is commended.'

Aristotle, Greek philosopher

'Hit me again, and I'll have you banned from the group.'

Nigel Smith, anger management counsellor

ACCORDING TO THE CHURCH, anger, or 'wrath', is a complex sin, often caused by one of the others. Pride can often lead to anger, as can envy, with its vengeful eyes burning into the object of its resentment. Avarice may easily lead to anger if it is frustrated or impeded in any way and equally, if lust is balked, this will lead inevitably to anger.

In the early 1990s, when the Soviet Union was splitting into its component states and Russia was becoming more open than at any time under either Communism or the Romanov Tsars, the opportunity was taken to examine how attitudes in the West and East had diverged thanks to division by the Iron Curtain. The journalist Vitali Vitaliev travelled from his Moscow home to the major cities of the West, asking fundamental philosophical questions of various strata of society. In England, he went to champagne-swilling social events such as Glorious Goodwood, the Henley Regatta, to punk band gigs in Wandsworth and to raves in Essex fields asking exactly the same questions as he would have done at home.

His enquiries were the types of questions that were considered as quite normal small talk in Russian gatherings.

He asked people from a wide range of ages, political affiliations and economic classes half-a-dozen questions including, 'Does your life have meaning?', 'Are you spiritually content?', 'Do you respect me?' and the one that gained more variations in response than any other: 'What makes you angry?'

Answers to this last ranged from 'The wicked price of a case of Krug' or 'The poor standard of service in Harrods these days' through the spectrum with 'My husband leaving the toilet seat up' and 'Ridiculous parking restrictions' to the socially conscious 'Rape' and 'Third-World debt'.

Do we complain about the price of a Krug?
Do we boycott a store when we receive bad service?
Do we stand-up to Third-World debt?
What is the point of getting angry?

**There's no point unless we
do something about it.**

We all have a different idea about what anger really is. We must have, because anger is a reactive emotion, and we all react differently to different degrees and to different things.

As Vitaliev's straw poll revealed, our perception of our own sense of anger, certainly here in the West, seems to range in meaning from mild irritation to outrage, taking in bored resignation along the way for good measure.

Imagine the scene: a traditional British, Church of England marriage ceremony. The beautiful bride is standing at the altar with her husband-to-be. Both are looking radiantly happy in their wedding costumes. Members of their two proud families fill the church. As pink-faced children in unusually neat little suits and frilly dresses pack the aisles, and as the organ strains of Mendelssohn fade away, the vicar conducts the congregation through the ritual words, and the female guests prepare their tissues to receive a few gentle tears of joy.

The ceremony bowls along nicely, and as the vicar gets to the bit about '. . . if anyone knows any reason why this man and woman should not be joined in holy wedlock, then speak now or forever hold thy peace', an angry young woman storms down the aisle, screaming in rage and dragging two small children, dirty-faced and sobbing.

She shouts extremely loudly: 'Yes, I know a few bloody good reasons why this bastard shouldn't be joined in holy wedlock with this stupid tart! This no-brain fuckwit can't keep his trousers on for as long it takes to say his own name! He's the father of these two poor little bleeders, he's been married to me for seven years, and last week he announced he's got that slapper, Tracy, on the checkout at Quicksave, up the duff. He's a no good, lying cheat.'

As the organ strains of Mendelssohn fade away, the vicar conducts the congregation through the ritual words, and the female guests prepare their tissues to receive a few gentle tears of joy.

And with that the bridegroom turns round and stares her full in the face. The bride stares at her groom in stunned silence. The congregation sit in stunned silence. They look at the groom. Then, as one, they look at the woman, and she says, 'I'm so terribly sorry. I must be in the wrong church. My mistake, entirely. Do please excuse me.'

We've all done it. Not quite to the extreme of that example, probably, but anger can be controlled as quickly as it can arise, despite what religious instruction might have us believe.

The Church associates anger with fire: smouldering, blazing and spitting and, even when it's icily cold, still burning. This is why religions associate anger with the Devil – Hell is an endlessly burning pit, anger burns, so anger is the heat generated by the Devil's Furnace. Anger as a sin is classified by the Bible as 'a disorderly outburst of emotion connected with the inordinate desire for revenge'.

The size of a man can be measured by the thing that makes him angry.

The character of a man can be measured by what he does with that anger.

But what is so wrong with a bit of revenge? Despite what any socially conscious Home Secretary might say, our entire judicial system is cemented together with the glue of revenge. In the Bible, Proverbs tell us 'revenge is sweet'. Sweet indeed, but let's not forget the old saying that revenge is also 'a meal best eaten cold'.

Anger, in the *Sin to Win* context, is a controlled emotion, not the hotheaded demon sitting on your shoulder. Anger is merely a thermometer reading of how hot is your desire to prove yourself right.

London taxi drivers are a notorious bunch who have their own peculiar ways of gaining retribution. One, who picked up a group of American tourists from an expensive hotel on Park Lane, was asked to take them to the *Mousetrap*, the long-running, Agatha Christie murder-mystery play in the West End. Along the way, the Americans made it known that their houses and apartments back home were much bigger and better than those they saw in London. They made it clear that their cars were bigger and better; their cuisine knocked spots of London's finest; and that they travelled everywhere first class. They were rich. Outside the theatre, the Americans were duly dropped off, and the cabby told them the fare was five pounds and fifty pence.

The tourists paid five pounds and fifty pence exactly, explaining that they don't tip cab rides in America. As they started towards the theatre entrance, the cabby called out to them, 'Enjoy your play. By the way, it's the policeman who did it.'

S A I N T   O R   S I N N E R ?

Who is the most angry footballer this country has ever seen? Could it be Eric Cantona, famed for his karate kick on a fan who had been taunting him with racist abuse? Or perhaps Lee Chapman, the Leeds footballer whose wife, Lesley Ash, was the subject of terrace chants concerning a liason with the above-mentioned Eric? No, it has to be Vinnie Jones who's done the best out of being angry. Since his feature film debut in *Lock, Stock and Two Smoking Barrells* Vinnie's acting career has seen him make it big in Hollywood with parts in films like *Gone in 60 Seconds*.

A pinch of anger sharpens the mind.

Office politics can be a mean-minded, petty business based on simmering anger and revenge, but there are ways to turn these into useful, career-boosting tools.

Office politics can be a mean-minded, petty business based on simmering anger and revenge, but there are ways to turn these into useful, career-boosting tools. It's much easier on the conscience to take someone's job or buy their business at a distress price if they've done something bad to you. In the London office of a large multi-national, an assistant head of a department became increasingly angry with his boss over trips abroad. Whenever a conference came up in an exotic location the boss would always go, but he would never provide any input to the preparation. He expected his assistant to prepare the necessary file notes, write a presentation speech and have made all the necessary overhead projection slides and handout literature. Only when a conference was in some God-forsaken hellhole or a rampant war zone did the assistant, who was doing all the work, ever get to go.

One trip came up to Paris. The assistant thought that possibly, as the boss had been there many times before, he might get his chance of a few days in the French capital. But no, the boss insisted on going and would the assistant have the files ready for him the night before departure so that he could glance at them on the plane? The files were ready. They contained a fine presentation package for the businessmen of Paris . . .

. . . Paris, Texas. Instead of half an hour on what their company could do for sales on the Cote d'Azure, the distribution systems of Aquitaine, or marketing opportunities in the Pas de Calais, they met the concerns of Stetson-hatted oil men and cattle ranchers. And just for luck, the assistant slipped a little something extra in the file.

Knowing full well the boss wouldn't even open the file until he was sipping his first complimentary cocktail in club class, the assistant popped in a cooking foil cut-out in the perfect shape of a 9mm automatic pistol.

THE SIN OF ANGER — DYSON

There are few more compelling examples of a firm appearing from almost nowhere and delivering a brutal blow to the incumbents of a mature market. Dyson took on Hoover, for goodness sake, a firm so well established that its name had long since become the generic term for its product. Vacuum cleaners have never been exactly sexy, but all of a sudden there was something new and special on the market. It was something that sucked extra hard, had no bag, and had a see-through middle to show off its unrivaled appetite for dust.

Hoover, still nursing a hangover from its ill-conceived free flight extravaganza, was horrified. It tried to produce something comparable, recognising that Dyson had quickly planted roots in its territory, but suffered the severe indignity of being slapped by the courts for copying Dyson's new concept. The big guy lifting from the little guy — it was supposed to be the other way around. Dyson feasted on its victory, transmuting its underdog status into a defining quality. It does old jobs in new ways.

James Dyson's company has turned over more than £3 billion as a result of his anger. He explains on his website that he often feels 'let-down by products and left with the feeling that I could have designed something better'.

That passion doesn't cool down when he leaves the R&D lab. Patenting his inventions, ranging from the 'ballbarrow' to the 'wheelboat' nearly bankrupted him. Now he campaigns to make it easier for people to protect their ideas.

When he was finally released by the Heathrow airport police after failing to pass through the X-ray machine, the boss made his way to Paris, a day late and still sore from a very personal search with a size eight rubber-gloved hand. He made a presentation that might as well have been intended for the people of Ulan Bator for all the difference it made to his Parisian audience.

Within two weeks, the boss was demoted to work alongside his assistant, but only for a few days. Who got the boss's job? The assistant, who shone when he was called over to Paris to make up for the first debacle. In this instance, anger had been used more as a tool of revenge than aspiration, but it had an unexpected and welcome side effect.

Anger wants revenge.
Anger won't let you put up with being messed about.
Anger wants the wrongs put right.

Use anger to find your peace.

There is another story, which may or may not be true. If it is true, I can't tell you for reasons that will become obvious after you've read it.

In the early 1980s, a female student graduated from college with top class qualifications in hotel management. She planned to start at a relatively lowly level to get a grasp of the grass roots of the business, but her ambition was to run an establishment and then to own a hotel by the time she was thirty. Her first job was with a large, provincial, privately owned hotel in the grand style. The owner considered himself to be in the same grand style and only took on a female as junior house manager on the basis that a girl would be neat and tidy, wouldn't make any waves and would bat her eyelids at the residents. He treated her pretty badly. He also ran the hotel pretty badly and it survived on misplaced enthusiastic listings in tourist guides and the fact that it was the only large hotel in town.

After about a year, our junior manager was looking for a promotion, with more responsibility and the chance to have more input in improving the business and possibly even a pay rise. The owner was unimpressed. He had no idea that his hotel was only just about surviving thanks to her efforts. He did give her more responsibility. He told her to take over running the cleaning and her first job was to cut back on staff. This meant that between shifts on reception, she was making beds and emptying kitchen waste bins.

She began to get angry. She knew she was right about her abilities and decided to do something about it. She gave one month's notice. But she didn't let her anger waste that month.

Edward III of England arranged to have his incompetent father Edward II assassinated in the nastiest way possible – by having a red-hot poker shoved up his royal throne.

SAINT OR SINNER?

Edward III of England plotted with his mother to have his incompetent father Edward II removed from the throne, which he did by arranging to have him assassinated in the nastiest way possible – by having a red-hot poker shoved up his royal throne. He then went on to arrange the assassination of his stepfather, Roger Mortimer, the man who had ruled England while Edward was a child, and confined his mother to her home for the rest of her life. Not a happy camper, our Edward.

T H E   S I N   O F   A N G E R   –   A P P L E

Apple, through all its ups and downs, has retained one distinctive feature – its bloody-minded determination to do things its own way. It has made a virtue out of angry resistance to the industry standard, to creeping homogenisation, to boring white boxes populating ever more densely the world's desktops. It has defiantly always promoted its own way of doing things and won loyalty and approval for this idiosyncrasy.

Things looked good in the early days before the company took a steep turn for the worse, but the return of co-founder Steve Jobs restored a sense of purpose and steered the firm back towards profitability. He reminded the world of Apple's capacity for innovation and design.

Colourful PCs, sleek laptops, and an unusual emphasis on style made the firm less vulnerable to the vagaries of an otherwise abundantly over-invested and over-supplied industry. iMac's, iBook's, the Apple operating system are all highly distinctive. Apple has thrived as the little guy against industry giants – originally IBM, then the multitude of other PC-manufacturers.

During those four weeks, rooms started to develop a bad smell. A serious, 'get the health officer in fast' type smell. First a room on the second floor, then another on the fifth, then after a while, all of them. Experts came and experts went. It was dead rats rotting in the air ducts. It was the sewers backing up. It was blocked drains. It was blocked toilets. It was a different theory every day. But it kept growing worse and worse until every room in the hotel stank. They were sprayed. They were fumigated. They were scrubbed with bleach. Nothing shifted the smell. What did shift, though, were the residents, who first left, then stayed away, in droves.

During that month, our junior manager/cleaner had been busy. Every time she emptied bins in the kitchen, she carefully extracted any prawns that had been left over. Each day while she was attending to the rooms, she took off the end of the old hollow brass curtain-rail and pushed in half-a-dozen prawns. Eventually, every room in the hotel had prawns in its curtain rail. Rotting prawns give off a stench like no other. A rotting prawn could make a rancid skunk swoon at twenty paces. The other scheme she got busy with was to see a few banks and investment houses.

When the establishment went into receivership, the news of its peculiar problem was well known in the business. The junior manger had made sure of that. It was considered unsellable and she bought it for no more than the price of a small terraced house. She had the curtain rails removed. She refurbished the rooms and there she was: owner of her own luxury hotel, which thrives to this day.

Religions have a particular downer on anger, due to its inflaming other sins and being comprehensively entwined with them. Richard Branson is one of those who use multi-sin techniques, but his anger often shines through. Back before the days of Virgin Atlantic, a friend of mine was having a business lunch with Branson in a boardroom overlooking the Thames, in London. Branson was there with a few of his senior aids to talk about setting up a new airline.

My informant had got Branson out to lunch, having quickly spotted an opportunity, and was in with the chance of beating off other suppliers of aviation services, with a view to gaining lots of new, potentially profitable business. As they chatted over their smoked salmon starters, my man noticed that Branson appeared distracted and then suddenly turned on one of his staff and said something to effect of 'What's that bloody boat doing there? Get it moved now!' He was plainly angry. He had been looking out of the huge panoramic windows and had seen a pleasure boat being moored in front of one of his. The view from his boat was obscured and he felt that this wasn't what he wanted. That wasn't the way it was meant to be. Most of us would have made a quiet note to get the situation sorted after lunch, a lunch that had nothing to do with his pleasure boat business. But Branson's anger made him act immediately.

His wrath also becomes apparent in his dealings with British Airways. Airlines are notoriously protective about their routes. Routes are their major asset. Seats are their products, but they are products that have almost zero shelf-life. Once a plane has departed with an empty seat, you can hardly sell it. The opportunity to sell that seat on that flight for £299 has gone forever.

Like a naughty terrier, [Richard Branson] yapped and nipped away at the ankles of the mighty British Airways until he got his own way.

BA is big, strong and powerful so, when they decided they didn't much like the idea of Virgin muscling in on their routes, they stopped it. Branson, unused to not getting his own way, and used to proving that he is right, vented his anger by suing BA through the courts. Like a naughty terrier, he yapped and nipped away at the ankles of the mighty British Airways until he got his own way. His legal argument was that he was breaking up old monopolistic practices and bringing cheap air travel to the masses.

Now that his airline is amongst the largest in the world, with shares held by Singapore Airlines and with his aircraft flying many thousands of long-haul profitable miles, Branson routinely angrily threatens legal action against those he feels are muscling in on his routes. This is what 'anger management' means here.

Anger, in the hands of a successful sinner,
is a concentrated dose of passion.

The passion to put things right.

Watch Branson get angry when he's criticised about the standard of service provided by Virgin Trains. He gets very angry. You think he's getting angry with Railtrack, for screwing up the track system, or at himself or his staff in frustration. But no. In fact, he is getting angry that someone even asked the question.

Take the top job. The most powerful job on the planet. The Presidency of the United States of America. One would have thought that to get to the Oval Office and rule the Free World, a president-in-waiting would need to be a great manager of people, analytical, fast thinking and, most of all, intelligent. One would have thought so, but history has taught us otherwise. Reagan and Bush Junior between them, at their peak and on a good day, were thick enough to make custard jealous. What every president really needs to get to the top is anger. By the bucket-load.

SAINT OR SINNER?

Angered by George Bush Jr's naming of his cat 'India', Hindu MPs struck on a highly amusing and appropriate form of revenge. A toilet in the centre of Calcutta's business district is to be called the White House. That's taking the piss successfully.

THE SIN OF ANGER – ASDA

Asda has channeled a fair bit of anger at its competitors over time, taking on the supermarket giants headlong over price – the battleground to which they all eventually descend. But the real focus of its aggression, albeit as part of the broader fights for market share, has been against the manufacturers of the brands it stocks on its shelves. Asda has made it its business to expose the margins of retailers, itself included, and then slash at them conspicuously to enhance its discounting credentials.

And when the brands complain about their methods, Asda takes off the gloves. It doesn't mind a scrap, as Levis discovered when the European court rejected the jean manufacturer's attempt to block Asda selling its goods at cut prices. Drug companies have also experienced Asda's refusal to back down. So it is no wonder that the store attracted the interest of the retailing world's ultra-discounter, Walmart. Pile 'em high, sell 'em cheap, and don't let anyone try to stop you. That's Asda's angry strategy to compete in the dirty discounting arena.

Bush Junior's father, the Republican President from 1989 to 1993, has been described as a self-made millionaire through Texas oil. Far from it. He was born to a wealthy New England family of bankers with a silver foot in his mouth, as we later discovered though his enigmatic speeches. But his frustration at not living up to the intellectual standards of his erudite father gave him anger. And anger supplied him with enough energy to succeed regardless.

As a 'Texan' oil man, and angry with the 'liberal left' wanting to stop the Vietnam War, he could afford to make huge donations to Republican Party funds. The Party, employing the Sin of Greed and playing on Bush's pride, appointed the witless wonder as the U.S. Ambassador to the United Nations. From there, through good-timing, generous donations, luck and lashings of self-belief, he worked his way through the role of Chief of Mission, U.S. Liaison Officer to People's Republic of China (this is a man with conservative intolerance of all things Communist ranging from the teachings of Chairman Mao through to men with long hair), Director of the CIA and, eventually, Vice President under Ronald Reagan, himself a star-gazing dreamer of such ineffectuality, that Bush's wrath kept him busy for eight long years until he could himself take over the reigns.

Let's not forget that Reagan consulted an astrologer before making any policy decisions, which led to Bush describing his budget policies as 'voodoo economics.' He was even angry with his own Republican boss. When the time came for Bush to run for President on his own in 1988, his loyalty to Reagan had robbed him of a separate identity, except in that one respect of anger. No one could describe the prematurely senile Reagan as 'angry'. Fortunately for Bush, he thus kept the support of party regulars and most Republican governors to win the nomination.

It was his good fortune to be opposed by a Democrat who appeared even less purposeful than himself: Michael Dukakis, the former Governor of Massachusetts. Bush unleashed a series of controversial ads and rumours that undermined Dukakis' stand on crime, questioned the mental health of the Governor's wife, and ridiculed his experience or lack of it, a mini-masterclass in using anger to gain advantage.

'Read my lips,' he said as if everyone listening was educationally subnormal...

Bush's first statement as President was on Federal Taxation, and he was irritated by anyone who had the temerity to question this tax policy. 'Read my lips,' he said as if everyone listening was educationally subnormal, 'No more tax hikes.' This was just before he put up taxes to fund his 'New World Order', or as we now call it, the invasion of Panama, or as we now call that, the rehearsal for the Gulf War. In the Gulf, he inspired his troops with his anger against Saddam Hussein, but it might as well have been any other foreigner he didn't like for all the difference it made. The Gulf and Panama were a godsend for Bush, whose natural anger was directed towards Russia and China, but who couldn't find any excuses to go to war against them.

The Gulf War raised Bush's popularity quotient to an unprecedented high of 90%. Bush's anger saw him through four years of presidency, overcoming his irritable vowel syndrome; his tax hike after having promised to never raise taxes; and his failure to articulate a consistent policy towards Eastern Europe. If ever anyone alluded to all these failings he simply went into Mr Angry mode and made blatant references to his Second World War heroism and to his dramatic victory over Saddam Hussein, as if he personally had been running through the streets of Baghdad blasting away with a bazooka.

When the Senate accused George Bush of practising nepotism in the White House, who was it that he angrily appointed to investigate the charge? His son-in-law.

When the Senate accused George Bush of practising nepotism in the White House, who was it that he angrily appointed to investigate the charge? His son-in-law.

On the foreign front, Bush sent U.S. troops into Panama to capture the head of that country's government, who had been indicted by a U.S. court for his role in a South American drug smuggling ring, despite his illicit support for the Contras. When Iraqi dictator Saddam Hussein invaded neighbouring Kuwait, an oil-rich and pro-American Arab nation in the Middle East, an act carbon-copying the invasion of Panama, Bush sent a force of 700,000 (largely American, but also including troops from twenty-one nations) to drive him out.

SAINT OR SINNER?

The accurately named General Butt Naked was one of the most bloodthirsty leaders in one of the most bloodthirsty conflicts of recent years, the Liberian civil war of 1989 to 1997. Butt Naked, real name Joshua Milton Blahyi, led his troops into battle wearing nothing but tennis shoes; allegedly sacrificed small children to gain invincibility; and became feared for his ferocity throughout the country. Unlike Generals No Mother No Father and Fuck Me Quick, Butt Naked made it through the war alive which is a matter for some celebration in Liberia.

Sadly, eventually, Bush's anger wasn't enough to secure a second term against the largely unknown Bill Clinton.

Clinton's lust was stronger than Bush's anger. Although, paradoxically, Clinton did keep up the tradition of enjoying his own bit of bush in the Oval Office.

How many successful people, with an impassioned personality, can you think of?

How many successful people, with a passive personality, can you think of?

George Walker, a former champion boxer and head of the Brent Walker leisure group, was worth £40 million when he went bankrupt owing £180 million. Walker's career was spurred on almost entirely by anger; the anger at being a poor East End boy. He began as a porter at Billingsgate market before he became a boxing star in the 1950s. With cash raised in the ring, he opened a nightclub called Dolly's in London and then, in 1969 bought a greyhound track, which was the start of Brent Walker. The business expanded to include the William Hill betting shop chain, Pubmaster, the tenanted pub company, and property that included the Trocadero in London and the Brent Cross shopping centre, claimed to be the first American-style shopping mall in Europe. Walker's empire collapsed in 1991 with debts of £1.2 billion. He was acquitted following a Serious Fraud Office investigation into the collapse of Brent Walker and is currently back in the City of London raising $15 million for the expansion of Premier Telesports, his Russian gaming business which at the time of writing he intends to float on NASDAQ with an expected value of at least $300 million. So how did someone who fell so far from grace, with a reputation in tatters, rise again?

As he tells it, he has that certain knowledge he is right. And he is always prepared to prove it.

Following his bankruptcy, he happened across an old business acquaintance, who at the time was running the European arm of the cigarette makers Gallagher's. They had lunch and began chatting about business opportunities. Gallagher's were concerned with falling cigarette sales and were desperately seeking expansion markets. Walker, with a little time on his hands, had been watching quite a lot of television. As this was the early 1990s, the screens were full of pictures of Eastern Europe. Walker noticed that a lot of these newly freed folk were smoking, and suggested that Gallagher's open an operation in Russia. No successful executive worth his salt wanted to go to Russia. So Walker said he would.

SAINT OR SINNER?

Vince Lombardi, the late Green Bay Packers coach, understood passion, enthusiasm and wrath. He was so ferocious that his players, men with brick walls for shoulders, feared him. 'When he said 'sit' you didn't look for a chair,' said one former player. His motto, 'If you're not fired with enthusiasm you're fired with enthusiasm', was learned at great cost by star offensive-line player, Jim Ringo. Ringo, once quoted as saying, 'I would rather be a lamppost in Denver than a dog in Philadelphia' was sold by Lombardi to the Philadelphia Eagles. His crime? Sending a lawyer to negotiate his contract.

Once he was there, and successfully helping all the ex-Communists to celebrate losing the shackles of the totalitarian state with doses of emphysema and heart disease, Walker noticed they would bet on anything. They would bet on two flies crawling up a beer glass, given half a chance.

Walker noticed they would bet on anything. They would bet on two flies crawling up a beer glass, given half a chance.

There was practically no horse racing in Russia, which had been considered a decadent affectation not worthy of the proletariat, but he knew a bit about betting. Back home, very few punters actually go the races. Most watch on television in betting shops. What difference did it make whether you were watching Newmarket in Birmingham or Goodwood in St Petersburg? They were still just horses on a television screen. Walker was back in the betting business, selling fags in the betting shops of course. And because he had to get horse and dog racing pictures beamed into Russia, he also has a firm hold on satellite television there.

If you ever challenge Mr Walker about his marketing morality – which I seriously suggest you don't, as he may be over 70 but still looks like a pretty mean light heavyweight – selling a killer drug and getting poor people hooked on gambling, he replies with all the control of someone who is angry inside but knows he is right. 'They want to smoke,' he says, 'let them have the same fags as we have'. 'They want to gamble, they need excitement.' He gets very angry indeed with the politically correct lobby. But then anyone who would move quite happily to a machine-gun protected compound in the outskirts of Moscow, a city where 'commerce' is spelt M-A-F-I-A, is hardly likely to be phased by some do-gooder columnist from the *Guardian*.

So successful have these new enterprises been, that Walker has now been discharged from his bankruptcy. Walker still carries himself with that East End pugnacity.

Angry – maybe, successful – certainly.

A surprisingly similar character to George Walker is Sir/Saint Bob Geldof. The archetypal post-punk angry young man has used his anger in a remarkably varied range of enterprises.

Working on the fringes of the music business, before the chart glory days of the Boomtown Rats, Geldof travelled to Canada where he worked at publishing music magazines. On his return home to Dublin, he was frustrated to find that setting up a business was almost impossible. He found an office, but when he asked the telephone company for ten lines he was laughed at. He moved to London, where the same happened. He developed the anger we've since seen displayed countless times. In expressing his anger with the world in which he found himself, Geldof formed the Boomtown Rats, a band representing the intelligent face of punk.

When their single, 'I don't like Mondays', redolent to the core of youthful anger and frustration, went to number one in the charts, were Geldof and his crew in celebratory mood on their triumphant appearance on *Top of the Pops*? No. Instead Geldof produced a glossy picture of John Travolta and Olivia Newton John, whom they had just knocked off the top spot, and proceed to tear it up in front of millions of adoring fans.

In 1984, aged thirty-two, Geldof was still the lead singer for his band, which had had several more big hits. After returning from a tour of the United States he found himself with a great deal of drive and energy but no concert schedule to fulfil. Nowhere to vent his anger. He sat down one night to watch television. A BBC documentary showed pictures of the Ethiopian famine. That part of Africa had seen no rain for three years.

In one scene, about 10,000 starving Ethiopians were trying to divide a single can of butter oil. It was decided that the first 300 might get just a taste. These scenes were exactly the red rag that the bull of his anger needed to be kicked into action.

Thousands of people were dying through starvation, and millions more might do so if some miracle of supply were not forthcoming. Bob Geldof made this miracle happen. He knew that government aid and the work of recognised charities would provide too little too late.

He got on an aeroplane and flew to Ethiopia to see for himself.

In one scene, about 10,000 starving Ethiopians were trying to divide a single can of butter oil. It was decided that the first 300 might get just a taste.

When he got back he composed a song called 'Do they Know it's Christmas?' with Midge Ure. Then he got on the phone. He succeeded in persuading the most famous British rock stars of the day to donate their time and talents to record it with him.

Duran Duran came. And Culture Club – Boy George and Jon Moss. And Sting and Wham! and, of course, The Boomtown Rats . . .

And Phil Collins joined them, and U2 and Bananarama and David Bowie and Frankie Goes to Hollywood and Heaven 17 and Trevor Horn, Cool and the Gang . . . And Marylyn and Paul McCartney . . .

And The Police and Nigel Planer and Spandau Ballet and Status Quo and The Style Council and Ultravox and Jody Watley. . . He rang every one of these and got very angry if anyone gave the slightest indication they might not join in. He got them all.

And they sang and played and recorded 'Do They Know It's Christmas? . . . Feed the World'. And it sold more copies than any record ever before in Great Britain. And it made over £8 million. And £8 million was given to relieve the famine in Ethiopia.

But that wasn't enough. For the next six months Geldof worked eighteen hours a day to create the greatest pop concert the world had ever known. He went to the Council of Europe and made them look stupid. He took on Margaret Thatcher in the street and his anger wouldn't let even her get away unscathed.

On 13 July 1985 the Wembley Stadium in London and the JFK Stadium in Philadelphia were linked by satellite. Seventy-two thousand people poured into Wembley and 90,000 into JFK. More than 50 top pop stars and groups took part, 1.4 billion people watched on television from 169 countries. As Geldof spat his anger into the television cameras, donations came in at the rate of £180,000 per hour. Live Aid made £70 million. And £70 million was given for famine relief projects in Mozambique, Chad, Burkina Fasso, Niger, Mali and the Sudan as well as Ethiopia.

What he said:

'People are dying NOW.'

'Halos get heavy and they rust.'

'The day I left Sudan was a good day, I only saw five people die.'

'Maybe I was given my arrogance and ego to do this.'

'Just give us your fucking money!'

'Live Aid became the focus of everyone's frustration and anger and shame. Very quickly it became a sort of phenomenon.'

Frustration and anger, that was what worked.

The Ten Commandments
of committing the sin of

ANGER

---

1 Anger is an anagram of range.

Anyone who has never felt the emotion of anger has never seen the full range of his or her talents. Like the mother who sees her child in mortal danger, unheard-of feats can be achieved on the wave of adrenaline that anger produces. Lift the car off your child – lift the lid off your self-constraint. Use that adrenaline.

2 Anger is a pointer to what you can achieve.

If something makes you angry, don't think, 'This is rubbish' without always thinking, 'I could do better than this' as well. You can. Your anger will let you. Bob Geldof gained the biggest television audience in history by using his anger. In the case of Live Aid, he didn't do it for personal gain. But he could have. And so can you.

3 Anger makes you feel better.

Edwin Stanton, Lincoln's Secretary of War, saw red mist when a general accused him of favouritism. Stanton complained to his boss, the President, who suggested that he should write a stiff, stern and sharp letter.

Stanton did so, and showed the letter, a strongly worded piece, to Lincoln. Applauding its powerful language, the President asked what he intended to do with it.

Surprised at the question, Stanton replied, 'Send it.'

Lincoln shook his head. 'You don't want to send that letter,' he said. 'Put it in the stove. That's what I do when I'm angry. It's a good letter and you had a good time writing it and feel better. Now burn it and write another one.'

4 Anger doesn't have to be negative.

Every charitable act ever committed is born out of anger: anger at injustice, or deprivation or social division. Anger is only ever negative if we try to ignore the cause of the problem.

5 Anger is a learning tool.

Learn from your mistakes. When you get angry with yourself, stop to think why. Why did you make the mistake? Why did you fail? Why didn't you do better? Use anger as a prompt to find excellence.

6 Anger is rarely the solution, but it can provide the solution.

Does your boss make you angry? Then learn to reason with him. Run through the conflicts that you feel affect your interpersonal co-worker relationship, and while you're doing that he won't notice how you're making sure he's on his way out. Keep that gun-shaped piece of tin foil handy.

7 Remember to be nice when you're angry.

There was a famous *bon viveur* who always carried a dead mouse when dining out. If he didn't much like a meal, or was on his uppers and wanted a freebie, he simply placed his dead mouse under the table or, in extreme circumstances, under the salad lettuce and would very politely and quietly point it out to the manager. Who says there's no such thing as free lunch?

8 Use other people's anger to your advantage.

Just like the political prisoner who suddenly loves the torturer who stops applying electric shocks through his genitals, if you find yourself with an angry customer, they will love you forever if you solve the problem that sent them into the rage. There are companies who, having got their customers through their metaphorical shop doors, deliberately make life difficult before then providing solutions to problems the customer never knew they had.

The trick is called 'squashy tomatoes' and originates from the greengrocer's trade, where it is passed on from generation of loveable rogues to generation of lovable rogues. That's where I learned it. We used to hide bags of rotten tomatoes at the back of our stall – tomatoes that we had either bought on the cheap or were going to waste. When the customer picked the good tomatoes off the stall, I was taught to switch the bags. Eleven times out of ten, the customer would come back the following week, complaining that the toms had gone soft by the time she got home.

As a third-generation barrow boy, I had the secret solution. The tomatoes are chosen, not switched this time, and I would put a 'freshness herb' leaf in as well. It's a bit of privet or something picked off a hedge. But the tomatoes didn't go squashy that week and the customer would come back every week to the one barrow boy who has the secret ingredient.

9 Anger provides a deadline.

An achievement is an aim that has met its deadline. Anger is a close relative of impatience. There's nothing like a good strong shot of anger to speed up your deadlines.

10 You must be yourself to be at peace.

You don't want to be yourself, you want to move on, you want to improve. So stuff peace and get angry.

Exercise on

ANGER

R emember that scale of 1 to 10 we talked about before? Playing from a 10 doesn't necessarily mean feeling happy and chuffed and picking wild flowers. It means being in a resourceful state – the state that is going to be most likely to lead to effective actions and the results that you want. Playing from a 10 can mean getting angry if you want to take action and get results. After all, the way to hell is paved with good intentions; we only get rewarded for our actions.

You already know some ways to conjure up a state from thin air, so you know how you can become angry (if you skipped the exercises in the revelations about Pride, then your piety is showing through . . . go back and start sinning). The key now is to control it and channel it to create action and results.

Have you ever been bugged by something, but somehow never got round to sorting it out? The reason is that we are governed by pain and pleasure. We will do things that give us pleasure and avoid things that give us pain.

For example, have you ever jammed rubbish into the swing bin – even though it is so full that the flap won't close and the week-old curry cartons on the floor around it are creating new forms of penicillin? You just can't be bothered to take the bin bag to the dustbin because the 'pain' of emptying the bin outweighs the 'pleasure' of having a tidy kitchen. Imagine now, however, that tonight is that hot date with Kylie, which you secured in the chapter on Pride. She's coming round for a candlelit dinner and she's promised to come commando. How might the pain/pleasure balance change now? The pain of emptying the bin might just be outweighed by the pleasure of Ms Minogue admiring your tidy kitchen, and commenting how she loves 'new men'. Result? One bin emptied in the time it takes Jimmy five-bellies to down a pint.

Here's a great way to flick that pain/pleasure switch. Follow these steps:

◆ Think of something that's been bugging you. Something you've been meaning to do, but just haven't been bothered to tackle. Don't choose something too big and hairy to start with – I don't want to get sued for creating a bunch of psychos who go and set fire to the Dome. But choose something that really bugs you: painting the shed, losing the beer gut, getting a pay rise . . .

◆ Use the techniques described in 'Pride' to get angry. I don't mean the kind of after-pub 'Are-you-looking-at-me?' angry. I mean the passion to put things right; steely determination – the kind of controlled energy where you think 'this matters and I need to damned well sort it out, NOW!'

◆ Ask yourself what are the consequences of not taking action? What will it cost me? What is the pain? Write down your answers. Think broadly – think about the financial pain, the emotional pain, the loss of face, the possible breakdown of relationships. Really ham it up. Think about the pain over the next week, the next month, the next year, the next five years. It is important that you do write your answers down, otherwise you'll just get in a stew here and now and may not carry this into tomorrow and beyond.

◆ Ask yourself, what are the benefits of taking action? What will I gain? What is the pleasure? How does that make me feel now? Again, write down your answers and think broadly – you want to associate as much pleasure as you can with taking action.

◆ Lastly, ask yourself, what do I need to do RIGHT NOW? What action can I take this instant that will start to make this happen? I don't mean what action can you take today or this week, I mean now. THIS INSTANT. Strike while the iron is hot. Put this book down and go and do that action right now. Start sinning and enjoy it.

The Sin of
AVARICE

'If you can actually count your money you are not really a rich man.'

J. Paul Getty

'Money isn't everything. Don't forget credit cards.'

Mrs J. Paul Getty

THE BIBLE'S VERSION OF AVARICE, sometimes referred to as covetousness, is that of the mean, niggardly, parsimonious miser who by his very nature is shut away from life. He sits at a table inspecting and drooling over his small mountain of gold coins. He embraces the coins and, as he runs his fingers through them, he revels in a sensual thrill from possessing and caressing so much physical wealth. He is alone with his money, and his money is his only source of comfort. The miser hides behind his pile of gold and makes it his protective shield against the world. He can think of nothing else but the near obscenity of his financial wealth. Lucky bastard.

Covet his wealth.

Spiritual wealth is all very well and good, but we all have an undying and necessary need for financial security. Thinking Godly thoughts and cleansing the mind of

The Church doesn't give up its wealth, nor its need and desire for wealth, and neither should you or I.

sinful inclination may have been all right for Mother Theresa of Calcutta, but it isn't going to keep the kids in new socks this term, let alone buy that new Lamborghini Diablo. It may be no use at all to be the richest person in Heaven, but who the hell wants to be the poorest person here on earth?

In this consumer society of the twenty-first century, our puritan religious leaders outwardly rail against the love of material wealth. The only corollary to that – the theory that the rich man who enjoys his wealth is a sinner – must be that the poor man who has nothing has been allocated an open season ticket to get him into Heaven. The poor man is a good man, and material wealth is a bad thing. So why doesn't the Church sell all its art treasures, all its gold and silver plates, all its antique pine pews, sell all the great bells in its towers for scrap and convert all its churches and cathedrals into homes for the homeless? People don't come much poorer than those who don't have a roof over their heads.

The Church doesn't give up its wealth, nor its need and desire for wealth, and neither should you or I.

There is only one person who tells you that money
isn't worth having and means it sincerely.

Your boss.

At first glance, the Sin of Avarice isn't a million miles away from the Sin of Envy. Quite simply, Envy is concerned with the desire for status and recognition. The Sin of Avarice is designed to reign back ambition.

No business would ever have got off the ground if it weren't for avarice. No invention would ever have been brought to market, no factory constructed, no coal dug out of the ground, no crop ever sewn. If everyone had stricly observed the rule against avarice since the beginning of time, we'd still be living in caves. And even that's debatable, because in the world where there is no material wealth, the man who has a cave to shelter his family is wealthy beyond measure, and he is committing the sin of avarice. There is no good logic to not committing the sin of avarice whatsoever. Nothing worth having was ever obtained without a good dose of coveting.

According to conventional religious wisdom, avarice is not so much the love of material wealth – the enjoyment of possessions – but more the love of merely possessing. To buy that second car we don't really need is seen as a love of possessing. To have a television set in the bedroom when there's a perfectly good one in the lounge, is the love of possessing. Presumably, to have that third child is to commit the sin of avarice. This is the Church itself sinning. The Church is committing the sin of envy. 'No one can need so many possessions or take any real pleasure from them,' they say. No? I think I'll be the judge of whether I want a Ferrari as well as an Aston Martin, a CD player as well as a MiniDisc or tea with sugar, thank you very much vicar.

Call me cynical. Call me lacking in faith. Call me guilty of heresy, but it seems to me that the Church's definition of a money grabber is anyone who grabs more of it than they do.

Again there is no logic to their argument other than envy, unless it is fear. When William Caxton brought the printing press to England and started mass-producing books in 1477, the Church tried to have this new business banned as the work of the devil. Until that time, all books, and with them, knowledge and religious truth, were the sole property of the Church, and indeed, the Church was the only organisation that made books. They wanted to hang on to this monopoly of printed information (or, in their case, misinformation), which is quite clearly a case of the Church committing the sin of avarice. And they were absolutely right to. The beginnings of the decline of religious observance and the questioning of received religious teachings right across Europe can be directly traced back to the printing of the first books.

'A fifty pound note has been found in the foyer. Would the person who lost it kindly form a queue at the manager's office.'

Notice pinned up in a theatre bar.

There's more to being covetous than just poring over your bank statements as a form of self-stimulation. The old cliché that 'money won't buy you happiness' is palpable nonsense.

As Caroline Aherne's alter ego, Mrs Merton, once asked in an interview with Debbie McGee: 'What first attracted to you to your husband, the millionaire Paul Daniels?' The love of money buys you other things that you love. It allows you to afford a wife and children and a nice big house to keep them happy. And if they are happy, you will be happy.

Let me make that a little clearer for you. Money does buy happiness.

Let me make that a little clearer for you. Money does buy happiness.

From reading this book, you may have deduced that I'm not the most politically correct man on the planet, and there's nothing more un-PC than declaring a love for the filthy green lucre. So let me explain. Money is a catalyst for making you happy and keeping you happy. Not having money is a catalyst for making you unhappy and keeping you unhappy. Not convinced? Pore over the divorce statistics – they're higher amongst poorer families. Check out domestic violence figures – there's no surprise as to which demographic group packs the punches. Take a look at life-expectancy data, data on alcohol abuse and drug-dependency. It's a crying shame, but it's also a fact.

There are exceptions to the rule. Many people who are born seriously wealthy lose the value of money, and with this they lose the happiness that it brings. Take Her Majesty Queen Elizabeth II as an example. She is one of the richest women in the world. She has a massive unearned income and a large army of servants to tend to her every need and whim. Sure, she has to go to work a few days a year, read the odd speech, open the occasional parliament and wave at the Ascot crowds from a horse-drawn carriage now and then, but she could retire tomorrow, let her son take over, and she still wouldn't run out of cash if she lived to be 150 years old. And yet look at her. She goes around the world attending banquets and grouse shoots with a face like a smacked arse. But she has never been poor.

The rest of us, who weren't born stinking rich, know very well that the serious accumulation of wealth, and its retention, will make life easier. And if life is a little easier, we'll be a little happier.

An important part of using the Sin of Avarice is knowing how to retain wealth. There are two things the European Royal families are very good at – strangling grouse and staying wealthy.

Why is it that we seem to hate success in others?
If we see someone succeed, we don't cheer for them.
We cry for ourselves.
Surely it's healthier, more rewarding,
and more positive to yearn after what they have,
to want what they have, to crave for what they have.

**Through coveting, we too could
have what they have.**

The nineteenth-century American, Cornelius Vanderbilt, recognised that it was easier to amass wealth than to hold on to it. He told his son, shortly before he died in 1877, that 'Any fool can make a fortune. It takes a man of brains to hold on to it after it is made.' His son seemed at first to have taken good note of his father's advice. In the eight years after his father's death, William Vanderbilt more than

S A I N T O R S I N N E R ?

Bill McCarthy, an associate professor of sociology at UC Davis, and Professor John Hagan of Northwestern University, recently published a study in the journal *Social Forces* suggesting that criminals would make the best businessmen. 'Some offenders score high on measures of competence, they're willing to work with other people and they make decisions that increase their earnings,' McCarthy said. 'We bear a considerable cost imprisoning people like this who could make a contribution in the legal economy.' It's official. Crime does pay.

doubled what was one of the largest fortunes the world had ever seen. William, in turn, died the world's richest man, with a fortune valued in today's terms of over $4 billion. Within thirty years his son, Neily, was nearly bankrupt.

At the time of Cornelius' death, the *New York Daily Tribune* commented that 'the ruling idea of Vanderbilt's later years was to amass a high fortune which should stand as a monument to his name, and make the head of the house a permanent power in American society. He chose one son out of many children and trained him alone to possess the inheritance of his vast wealth, as a King's first born is educated only for the crown [this is an American writing] and this favoured son he doubtless expected to transmit the deposit unimpaired and perhaps increased, to the head of the next generation.'

U.S. law and customs make no provision for such preferences and have never favoured the channelling of such wealth along a single narrow avenue. There is no country in the world where fortunes can be amassed so quickly, and yet there is no other where ancestral wealth is so rare.

THE SIN OF AVARICE – AMAZON

Online retailers were the ultimate in covetous businesses. They started from nothing and tried as quickly as possible to infiltrate established market-places, often dominated by stodgy and unreconstructed old businesses. Most of them failed famously in one of those joyously rare moments business history when everyone knows something isn't right, but they somehow manage to suspend that disbelief for long enough to indulge a grossly speculative bubble. Amazon, at least for the moment, looks to have been an exception – a business that has made a success of its covetousness.

Amazon started out in 1995 selling books over the Internet, competing with traditional book retailers. Then it set its sights on the music business, DVDs, videos and more or less anything that could realistically be delivered by conventional mail services. Initial success relied on speed – it had to penetrate its customers' online consciousness before anyone else to thrive in an unprecedentedly flighty market. However, it established itself as one of the most efficient online retailers, cemented some form of loyalty from its customer base, and pulled through the first wave of the dotcom meltdown.

It's the classic story of a business exploiting a new distribution channel to get its grip on other players' customers. Covetousness.

The decline of the Vanderbilts over the following years reinforced this notion. However, those who practiced avarice, the Du Ponts, Pulitzers and Rockerfellers, remain powerful in society today.

Calouste Sarkis Gulbenkian was, at the time of his death in 1955, one of the richest men in the world. Having had made his pile in industry, he philanthropically endowed the international Gulbenkian Foundation for the advancement of the arts, science and education. He wasn't born into wealth, but he coveted it, and a philanthropist he may have been, but he still knew how to spend his own money for his own enjoyment. One day, he decided to buy a Rolls Royce. Driving it out of the showroom, he was asked by an admiring passer-by what he thought of his new purchase. He replied 'It has a silky-smooth engine, a Connolly hide interior, and the brakes are of such quality, they tell me the car can stop on a sixpence, whatever that is.'

Some of us are born with a silver
spoon in our mouths.
Some of us get a better chance in life
through education.
Some of us are born into wealth.

**In the currency of self-made success,
we are all born poor.**

One-time U.S. presidential candidate Ross Perot made his fortune by selling computer services and then speculating with his cash. He sold his original company Electronic Data Systems to General Motors in 1984 for $1 billion. GM gave him a further $700 million when he left the board and reduced his shareholding. And yet, Perot became the first person in history to make and lose a billion dollars in less than two years. Between their issue in 1968 and March 1970 the value of his shares in EDS went from $150 to $1476 million. In the next three months, the share price dropped from $4164 to $33, making a loss of $1179 million. In those twelve weeks, Ross Perot was losing $74 a second, every minute of every day.

As I said earlier, I'm not the most politically correct bloke, but I try. Quite rightly, and speaking as a Jewish man with Scottish roots, I believe it's no longer big, clever or funny to make jokes about personal traits based on ethnicity. The tight Scotsman and the mean Jew are forever confined to the gagster's waste-paper bin.

So, this Norwegian, let's call him Jock Goldberg, is so mean that he refuses to employ a window cleaner. Rather than shell out the few pounds it will cost him to bring sunlight dancing through crystal clear panes into his gloomy house, he does the job himself, with a ladder borrowed, naturally, not bought, from a neighbour. At the top of the ladder, Jock Goldberg reaches out to a far corner of a bedroom window to remove a smear, and a fifty pence coin falls from his pocket. He finishes the job and gets to the foot of the ladder before it hits him on the head. That evening, his son comes home from school and proudly declares that he saved forty pence that day by running home behind a bus. His father scolds him. He should have run home behind a taxi and saved a fiver.

SAINT OR SINNER?

Even though she had stolen nearly $250,000 over a three-year period from her employer, Elizabeth Randolph Roach, 47, received a sentence in May of only probation, because a judge in Chicago sympathised with her shopping addiction, which he characterised as 'self-medicat(ion)' for severe depression. Roach used the stolen money to pay for 70 pairs of shoes, a $7000 belt buckle, and other clothes and accessories she purchased on trips to London, most of which she never wore.

These rotten old jokes are born out of envy. The ability to make money and hold on to it is to be admired. The ability to hold on to money is the ability to make more money.

Being avaricious, or covetous, involves not only loving our possessions, it also means having a desire for possessions that we do not yet have. Possessions other people have.

Success takes hard work, a good idea and self-belief.
More than that, though, success needs drive and ambition.

Successful people covet success.

Now in his seventies, Bernie Ecclestone is a success. The one-time racing driver has proved himself in the hard world of business. He is a self-made man – every penny of his £2.5 billion fortune is down to his own efforts. He is richer than the Queen, indeed he is richer than any other Briton, and is one of the highest-salaried businessmen in the world.

Bernie Ecclestone may not be a big man – at 5ft 4in – but he is the most important component of Formula One. He owns Formula One Holdings, which controls almost every part of the motor sport. He pays himself around £60 to £70 million a year and is expected to become several times richer if the company is floated on the Stock Exchange, a possibility which has been on and off for years.

One of the company's main assets is its 25-year contract with the sport's governing body, the Fédération Internationale de l'Automobile (FIA), to sell television rights. In an interview, Mr Ecclestone said that his determination to proceed with the sale of the company was driven by fear that the business could fall into the wrong hands when he retired or died. But he doesn't seem to want to let go. Why would he?

Mr Ecclestone has spent £70 million and 30 years of his life building up Formula One. Now, much of the company is owned by his wife, the Croatian-born Slavica who, at 37 and a 6ft 2in blonde bombshell and former Armani model, is obviously well qualified for the job.

He said: 'I would hate to see it go down the drain because it was badly managed. If all the teams owned it they'd destroy it. They can't agree on anything, not even on how to share their money out. They think they can run the business – I know they can't.'

Ecclestone built up his fortune, centred on his involvement in Formula One Holdings, which controls most aspects of Formula One motor racing throughout the world, from a conventional beginning. He graduated from Woolwich Polytechnic in south-east London with a degree in chemical engineering. But as a lab technician, he wasn't getting the things he desired. South-east London was pretty drab place in the 1950s. Frankly, it's not exactly Copacabana Beach during carnival time in the twenty-first century, but one of the few industries that thrives there is the second-hand car business. So, he became a businessman, enjoying success with a car and motorcycle dealership in Bexley, Kent. His car business brought him into contact with motor racing at nearby Brands Hatch, which in those

THE SIN OF AVARICE – PWC

The comical awkwardness of its name alludes to the covetousness of PricewaterhouseCoopers, an amalgam of Price Waterhouse and Coopers and Lybrand in 1998. But it isn't the merging of two giant accounting firms to produce the world's largest that represents the group's greed. It is its insatiable ambition to extend the range of its present professional services into every corner of the business firmament – the quest to provide the complete solution.

PWC isn't the only covetous accountancy firm in the game. Increasingly, they are all increasingly as culpable as one another. But it is the largest and that's how it qualifies for this spot. The company's 2000 results demonstrate just how far it has already infiltrated its tangential markets, with only about 40% of its revenues coming from traditional accounting and auditing services.

It has become a diversified conglomerate, surfacing everywhere from Tblisi to Mexico City and beyond. The buzz-word is multi-disciplinary practice. Every new bit of business, every new service is a networking opportunity. You start out doing a lowly audit and before you know it you are telling the board how it should reshape the business. Why let someone else, a McKinsey, get the consulting revenues when you can do it yourself with a modest extension to your core competencies. There isn't a professional service the big five don't covet.

days still ran alternate British Grand Prix. He became a moderately successful racing driver before a crash ended his hopes of competing at the highest levels, but he coveted other winning drivers and teams, and so he bought the ailing Brabham racing outfit. When Brabham rose to be the best in the sport, with the then best driver, Nelson Piquet, Ecclestone used his covetous nature to acquire, then nurture and protect his assets.

At the Monte Carlo Grand Prix his driver, having made the fastest time of the day in practice, sat back, hoping his pole position for the race wouldn't be taken by one of the other drivers. This was unlikely, but there was still plenty of timed practice left. Ecclestone wasn't content merely to sit back and hope – he made damn sure. He ordered his pit crew to fill up Piquet's car with all the right fluids – oil, water, brake cooling fluid – but all filled to above the required amounts, to the extent that liquids were sure to leak out under the pressure of a high-revving 1100 b.h.p. turbo-charged racing engine. He then sent Piquet out for a few fast laps along the racing line, with the result that his car deposited a fine coating of lubricants and water exactly on those parts of the track where every car would have to brake and turn in order to beat his time. No other car could even get close on the slippery surface and Piquet's pole position was assured.

Mr Ecclestone has enjoyed the benefits of being a highly successful executive – he owns homes in Corsica, an Alpine ski resort and has a villa on the French Riviera. Subscribing to the Sin of Avarice, he goes to extraordinary lengths to protect his benefits.

Knowledge is one of the most important
assets you will ever earn.

Avarice is the skill of hoarding assets.

**Most people forget up to 80% of what
they learn in 24 hours.**

THE SIN OF AVARICE – McDONALDS

It's not a good time to be running a business built around beef. In Europe, demand for red meat has collapsed in recent years, as consumers have taken fright at the seemingly endless stream of scares. BSE, foot and mouth, e-coli. None of them do much to boost the reputation of beef, particularly set against an underlying trend away from red meat.

So it's no wonder that McDonald's, the biggest burger seller in the world, has grown increasingly covetous of some of its less immediate competitors – purveyors of healthier foods. It has acknowledged the need to change its ways, if it is to grab hold of other people's clientele and stretch its interests beyond the deep fat fryer.

The first step has been to diversify its own menu – adding a larger share of non-beef products. Chicken McNuggets and Filet-o-Fish were the original new boys, but they have become more adventurous of late with the introduction of pork products and even the McChicken Keema Naan.

But it's still not enough. The golden arches are still anathema to the more militantly delicate fast-food customers. So McDonalds has acted even more radically to effect its covetousness. First, it bought a share of coffee chain Aroma, determined to grab a bit of the rapidly expanding brown bean market. And then, more dramatically, it bought a share of the ostentatiously wholesome sandwich vendor Pret a Manger. In the US it has also invested in Chipotle Mexican Grill and the Donatos Pizza chain.

McDonalds has decided that if it wants a piece of someone else's business it has to buy into their market.

One of the British Labour Party's promises in the lead-up to the 1997 General Election was a pledge to support a ban on tobacco advertising on Formula One cars. The major proportion of income for most teams was from the tobacco giants. Ecclestone gave the Labour Party a gift of £1 million.

Of course, there is no need to ban tobacco advertising on racing cars, no one buys cigarettes as a result. This isn't me speaking; it's the tobacco industry. That's why they each donate $100 to $200 million, and more, a year to have cars painted like fag packets. Not to sell cigarettes. Convinced? No, me neither. Tobacco companies understand avarice. They like a nice bit of protection of their markets too.

A European Community directive, in a bid to remove cigarette advertising from all sports, sparked the plan to ban advertising. Formula One was certain the ban would cost it dearly and mooted a move of all Grand Prix, normally held in Europe to the Far East, where several countries were keen to host the events, and, purely coincidentally, where less healthy and safety conscious governments don't interfere with the public demand for cigarettes.

Ecclestone went to Downing Street to explain the dire effect of the ban on British industry.

Ecclestone went to Downing Street to explain the dire effect of the ban on British industry.

In the meeting Mr Ecclestone said that Formula One, as a civil servant recalling the meeting descibes it, 'has put a lot of effort in to developing television.' Mr Ecclestone went on to say that 'digital technology was coming' and if Formula One went 'television will go with the races'.

Ecclestone might not have mentioned that in addition to controlling Formula One, he controls the rights to the television broadcasts that go with it.

When the news broke in the British press of Ecclestone's gift, his money was returned. It would take a conspiracy theorist of the first order to suggest that he was instrumental in the leaking of this news, but it did him no harm at all, either by reputation or financially.

When Silverstone, the traditional home of the British Grand Prix, was being a bit slow about updating its facilities, Ecclestone moved its 2000 race date from the usual summer weekend to early spring. When the car parks turned to bogs in the inevitable torrential English rain, and supporters by the thousand were unable even to reach the circuit, Ecclestone's point had been made. He wanted his asset protected and Silverstone hadn't been helping.

Ecclestone puts no limit on his material desires. On graduating from college, he had good qualifications but no money, so he went into the car sales business. From that business he went into motor racing. He treated that like a business, rather than the sport it had been up until that time. From driving, he went to ownership, and from owning a team he went to owning the entire business, which he now calls a sport.

To covet is to take the limits off your desires.

One of Ecclestone's most successful drivers, the Brazilian Nelson Piquet, was on a plane flying to London from his Monte Carlo home. As is the case with most celebrity customers, airlines like to make a fuss to show off to their other passengers and to bathe in their reflected glory. So, Piquet was invited up to the flight deck to chat with the pilot. Like most Formula One drivers, Piquet had his own private aircraft, which he flew himself, and during the small talk told by the pilot how he'd just taken delivery of a new Bell Jet Ranger Helicopter, which he kept for local trips from his apartment around Monaco and along the Côte d'Azure. 'But where do you find the space to land a helicopter in Monte Carlo?' enquired an incredulous pilot. 'On my yacht, of course', came the reply from the Brazilian three-times world champion.

Aspiring young race drivers were taught how to grow an unfashionably bad moustache, trim hedges and look miserable.

When the Birmingham-born, British driver, Nigel Mansell, attained his one and only world championship, he moved to the Isle of Man, built a new bungalow around which he planted a fir-tree hedge and, for a hobby, became a Special Constable. When his racing career ground to a halt, he started the Nigel Mansell Racing School, where aspiring young race drivers were taught how to grow an unfashionably bad moustache, trim hedges and look miserable.

There is a story about an elderly man, well into his eighties, who, in about 1996, arrived in London from Eastern Europe. He had obviously done well from the recently freed-up markets there. He wore fine clothes, a small amount of tasteful jewellery and was exceptionally well groomed, but he was, without doubt, very old. On his first day in the West End, he pitched up at high-class brothel in Shepherd Market. What could an octogenarian want in a high-class brothel? A meeting with Lord Archer, perhaps? No, this place was far too classy.

When the door was opened, the Madame looked slightly surprised as the old man said: 'I'd like to see Mary, please.' The Madame explained that Mary was their youngest, fittest and most expensive girl and that she cost £1000 a session.

'That's fine,' he said.

On day two, the same thing happened. He arrives, the Madame explains again that Mary is expensive at £1000 a go, and wouldn't he be happy with an older, cheaper model? No, he wants to see Mary. Later that day, the Madame and Mary get chatting. They discuss how rich this man must be, to able to afford a grand a day on something that lasts about two minutes at most.

On day three, he arrives yet again. The same routine happens, but by this time Mary is becoming fascinated by him. 'You must be very wealthy, man?' she enquires.

'Yes, I am', he says, 'I have my own import-export business which has prospered in the last few years.'

'And your accent,' says Mary, 'where do you come from?'

'Budapest,' comes the reply.

'Budapest?' says Mary, 'I have a sister in Budapest, who's in the same business as me. Do you know her?'

'Yes I do,' says the man, 'she gave me three thousand pounds for you.'

Enough is never enough.

The Ten Commandments
of committing the sin of

AVARĬCE

---

1 Thou shall not covet thy neighbour's ox.

And that's it. You don't need an ox. But covet away merrily thy neighbour's wife, his manservant, his maidservant, his car, his stereo, his au pair and everything else that is his that might be worth having. It's healthy. He wants you to covet it. That's called competition, and competition is healthy. If you can't get his possessions directly, then get better ones. When Ford wanted to improve their image by buying Ferrari to win the sports car championships in the 1960s, and Old Man Ferrari refused to sell, they didn't sit back. They got something that potentially was as good, in the Lola Mk 6, made it better and went to Le Mans and beat Ferrari on the track. In a bid to survive, Ferrari then had to be taken over by Fiat, who subsequently saw only two short periods of success until the late 1990s. When Fiat saw Bennetton winning everything, they coveted their driver and technical director and they took both. World championships followed.

2 Covet thy neighbour's business.

Some years ago, a good mate of mine was working in a business where there were two main suppliers. He and his competitor had roughly half the market each.

Naturally, as a covetous chap, my pal wanted more of his competitor's business – specifically one big customer who alone accounted for more than 10% of the market. But he could never get in. He used to make calls, had the occasional lunch and was always well received, but he never got the business. He couldn't work out how it was done until the second generation of answer phones came on the market. His new machine arrived, complete with a small pocket-sized device that generated a tone. When you were away from the office, you rang your own machine and placed the device over the receiver. The tone generated allowed you to hear your stored messages.

During the next round of contract negations, he bought a Stylophone. (For those of you too young to remember, this was a cheap, hand-held musical organ promoted with gusto by Rolf Harris. It generated a range of tones.) During one of his competitor's long lunch breaks, our man rang his office. The Stylophone was placed close to the receiver and the Stylus run along the keyboard until he heard the answer phone click into replay mode. And with that click, came all he needed to know.

3 Thou shall not covet thy neighbour's wife and get found out.

From listening to his competitor's messages, my frustrated friend learned that his competitor was having an affair with the customer's wife and business partner, who was passing on price bid information that always made sure he could put in a lower, later price.

It was a simple matter to record one of the juicier messages and then replay it to the buyer's answer phone. You can work-out the next bit for yourself, but the end result was that his competitor not only lost 10% market share but also was never going to get the chance to bid for it again.

4 Anything worth coveting is worth keeping.

Never give anything away. Most truly successful businessmen don't do interviews and when they do, they say nothing. In writing this book, I've interviewed CEOs from the Royal Bank of Scotland, Direct Line, First Direct, Channel 4 and Virgin. They all seemed like nice people. Clever, relaxed, happy, confident. They all gave up their afternoons to speak to me, but I was left with the feeling that I hadn't learned much.

Next time a business leader is being interviewed on radio or television, listen closely. Sure, a lot of words come out, but listen carefully to them. What did they actually tell you? What did you actually learn from it? Bugger all, probably. If you know things, don't give the information away. It's valuable. Don't leave important information on your answer phone if some else can access it.

Free information is only given away by people who don't know how to use it properly. Possessions that are worth coveting are only given away by people who don't know how to keep them.

5 As you covet something, so do others.

There was a small but explosive economic boom in Britain during the 1960s. Riding on the wave of swinging London and the Mop Top Fab Four, there were plenty who became rich beyond their wildest dreams. This was due, largely, to better mass media communications. Thanks to television, radio and magazines, people saw things they wanted. They started to covet things they had never seen before.

In true *Sin to Win* entrepreneurial spirit, there was a man who recognised that as he coveted, so too did many others. However, he was no pop singer; he couldn't play a guitar or write a number one best-selling concept album. In today's world, those talents (or lack of them) would guarantee any warbling girl/boy band a number one spot, but this was the 1960s. Fortunately for our entrepreneur, he knew people who could perform on stage. Not personally, but he didn't let that get in his way. He wanted their lifestyle and he used other people's same desire for that lifestyle to make a tidy profit, which he now lives on, some 35 years later.

6 Covet thy neighbour's information.

Our 1960s man went to see the Rolling Stones at a dance hall in south London. He paid his ten shillings to get in and found the place so crowded he could just about hear the band, but he certainly couldn't see them. He fought his way to the door and got chatting with the manager, 'I can't see the Stones', he complained.

'I'm not surprised,' replied the manager, 'they haven't arrived yet. In fact I don't think they're going to make it.'

'What's wrong? Has their van broken down?'

'I've no idea,' said the manager, 'I haven't booked them.'

The music that was belting out was the warm-up support act. An apology that the Stones couldn't make it went out later, and half the ticket money refunded to anyone who was sober enough to complain once the over-priced bar had run dry.

7 Thy neighbour's coveted information is thy information.

The following week, the beginning of February 1966, an advert appeared in the *Melody Maker*:

Rolling Stones Concert
Wembley Stadium
30th October
Tickets 25 shillings.
send postal order to . . .

If you haven't worked out who placed the ad, you haven't been paying attention. You haven't coveted all this information.

Our man got in excess of half-a-million postal orders for 25 shillings. That's over £625,000 in 1966 money; when a new car cost £600 and a three-bedroom semi would have set you back £3000. It was serious money. It had to go back, of course, when a second ad appeared in early October cancelling the concert, which had never been arranged.

8 Covet even if you have to give back.

Even though the cash had to go back to punters to stay within the law as it then stood, the interest alone on £625,000 was worth about £20,000, or a new house, a new car and plenty left over to enjoy the pop-star lifestyle. Just one of those extra thousand pounds left in even a modest interest-bearing account would today be worth over £1 million.

9 Covet thy neighbour's house.

It might be his factory, or his shop or his business, but make sure you take a good covetous look at it. A home-owner lived in a semi-detached property, which was one of two that had been converted from one larger, grander house. He wanted to buy the adjoining house to restore the property to its Georgian splendour. Coincidentally, thanks to the quirks of the house-price boom, one up-market house was worth more than two smaller ones. Second buyers had capital. Entry level, aspiring homeowners had none and couldn't get enough to raise the deposit for a mortgage.

Our house-owner didn't tell his neighbour he wanted to buy the house. That would have made him a specialist buyer, but instead, he did let it slip over the garden fence that houses of their type were about to collapse price-wise. The neighbour wanted to capitalise on his investment before it went down the drain and so put his property on the market at £100,000. The first person to view offered £95,000; the second £85,000; the third £77,000 and so it went on. When the seller realised the market was crashing, he went back to the first offer, which by then had gone down to £75,000. To help him out our friendly neighbour put in a bid of £80,000, which was eagerly snapped up. All the bids had come from friends of the friendly neighbour.

10 Coveting stops you becoming complacent.

A New York taxi driver once said, 'I see more of what is going around me because I'm not concerned with finding a parking space. It's not my business to stop and get out, I just keep driving on and seeing new things.'

The Sin of Avarice stops you from stopping. It keeps you driving on, seeing new things.

Exercise on

AVARICE

W e've already talked about our feelings or state of mind and how they can affect our behaviour and results. There is another layer lurking beneath this, which we need to understand in order to make avarice work for us. Beliefs.

Beliefs are the rules by which we live our lives. It's not my business to tell you which beliefs are 'right' or 'wrong', I'm only interested in which are useful and which are limiting. Limiting beliefs are the ones that are going to stop you from getting what you want, stop you from achieving your goals and stop you from enjoying your life.

How do you spot a limiting belief? To start off with, simply notice whenever you use the phrase 'I can't'.

'I can't dance.'
'I can't sell.'
'I can't imagine that happening.'
'I can't talk to my boss about it.'
'I can't be bothered.'

Sometimes 'can't' is craftily disguised with 'I am' – as in 'I am a poor negotiator' or 'I am no good with numbers'.

Take a couple of minutes to list out your 'can'ts'.

Now look down the list and ask yourself. Is that true? You can't? Really can't? There's absolutely, physically no way that you can do anything on that list? Full stop? End of story?

I doubt it. Ninety-nine times out of one hundred, 'I can't' simply means 'I simply won't entertain the possibility; I just don't believe it'. Beliefs are powerful things; we live and breathe by them, so how do we get them? The answer is that they are fed by past experiences: what our parents have told us; what our teachers have told us: the results we have achieved to date; what the media says. Beliefs give us a nice, cosy sense of certainty about how the world is and we tend to resist any suggestion that this certainty might be misplaced.

If you want to be avaricious – to have that eager desire to gain and succeed, your 'can'ts' will stop you. The scary thing is, they are often subconscious. In one of our coaching sessions there was a woman who wanted to be a top salesperson. She put in the hours and went to the meetings, but she had a real problem about cold-calling – it made her feel uncomfortable and threatened and she couldn't figure out why. After a bit of detective work we uncovered the problem. From an early age she'd been taught to believe 'I can't talk to strangers, because strangers might be dangerous.'

A useful belief when she was in pigtails walking home from school, not so useful fifteen years on. Her limiting belief was hindering her avarice to succeed. Do you remember in the chapter about gluttony we talked about how once you focus on something your mind becomes more aware of it? Remember the example of moving house and suddenly seeing loads of for-sale signs that you hadn't noticed before? That process is useful here too. Once you tune your brain to start looking for limiting beliefs, you'll start to realise you have stacks of them – you'll start to notice even the subconscious ones.

You might find that just noticing them will help to make your limiting beliefs disappear. However, you might also find that your reaction is something along the lines of:

'Well, it's a real shame, but I must be realistic – I honestly can't dance.'

If so, start questioning how you came to have that belief. Did a dance teacher tell you? Did you humiliate yourself at your first school disco? Is your dad a bad dancer (and they all are, believe me)? You may well find that the reasons really aren't that strong.

If you're still stumped, here's a powerful way to change beliefs:

You remember the exercise about biting a lemon? And the discovery that the brain can't tell the difference between what is real and what is imagined? Well, it is simple. If you imagine vividly enough that you are a fantastic dancer, that's going to give you a massive step forward in learning to dance.

You don't believe me? Well, let's take this thing about imagination a step further. Make a list of 'can'ts' that are limiting society as a whole. Don't worry, I'm not going to ask you to hold your hands together for world peace and hum, let me give you an example to show why this is useful.

Roger Bannister lived in an age where the medical profession believed it was physically impossible to run a sub-four-minute mile. In fact, if you were to attempt it, your blood would boil and your heart would explode. We may have slightly less respect for doctors since the activities of a certain Harold Shipman, but back in the 1950s what doctors said was believed absolutely by the rest of the population. Would you have attempted the four-minute mile with this belief system kicking around?

How did Bannister summon up the courage to challenge this belief? Firstly, he had the advantage of being a member of the medical profession. He was able to question some of the 'reasons' it put forward. Secondly, he was an early advocate of 'mental rehearsal' i.e., using his imagination to make himself believe he had already accomplished the feat and thereby making it easier to do in reality. He later said that when he broke the record he had already imagined the race happening hundreds of times in his mind's eye.

Funnily enough, as soon as Bannister broke the record, everyone's reference points were changed. The impossible became possible. Within a year numerous athletes had also broken the barrier.

Envy means not settling for second-best. Avarice means not settling for best. Don't let your personal 'can'ts' and even society's 'can'ts' hold you back.

The Sin of

SLOTH

'Idleness is only the refuge of weak minds.'

Lord Stanhope, 4th Earl of Chesterfield

'All I wanted was an afternoon off to go to my mother's funeral.'

Jim Scragg, servant to Lord Stanhope

SLOTH, IN OUR EVERYDAY LANGUAGE, means being reluctant to work or exert oneself, so it's not difficult to understand why the Church should have been quite so keen to include it in the list of Seven Deadly Sins. When all societies in Western Europe were ruled by the Church, the clergy needed the masses to work and to work pretty damn hard all the hours their God had – in his most infinite wisdom and generosity – kindly given them, to supply the Church with taxes and labour to build its places of worship. In turn, these massive structures, which in some cases took hundreds of years to complete, were used to strike terror into the hearts and minds of the workers to keep them slaving, paying taxes and, on pretty regular occasions, forming armies to go off to strange foreign lands to fight the infidels and give those people the Christian love of God, Holy salvation, the benefaction of the Lord, and syphilis.

Simple idleness in our terms seems fairly innocuous. We all need a day off now and again to recharge our batteries, have a lie-in and read the papers in bed over tea, toast and marmalade and that surely can't sound like much of a Satanic sin to even the most zealous fundamentalist Bible basher? To take an idle stroll, to window shop, to saunter about with no particular purpose and then linger over a drink at the pub with friends – how is that the road to Hell? It may not be the direct road to Hell, but it is certainly the first step on the side street leading directly to Hell Fire Avenue, if our religious leaders are to be believed. The work ethic, as instilled in us over centuries by the teachings of the Church, relies not only on us all working hard, but being seen to be working hard. Over time, this has become muddled and now, to be seen to be working, is itself the Holy Grail. Whether or not this work is to any great effect has become wholly irrelevant.

How many employers want their workers at their desks or workbenches at a fixed time in the morning? Most of them. Why? To get the full whack of work out of them? No. It's because they still confuse being seen to be 'at work' with 'working'. And this confusion arises from sloth being made a sin.

Do you live to work or work to live?

**The successful person, who understands
the power of sloth, does both.**

The dire consequences of the occasional burst of simple, pleasurable idleness had to be exaggerated because the masses might have learned to like it. If they had learned to like it, they might learn to want more pay for less work, and less work meant less time at work, and less time at work meant paying more people more money to fulfil the same output. It was in effect the fabrication of sloth as a sin that led to the formation of Trades Unions. Without the Sin of Sloth, there would have been no Tolpuddle martyrs, no General Strike and no Arthur Scargill.

Okay, but two out of three isn't a bad strike rate.

In its terror of workers deciding that they liked a spot of leisure now and again, the Church re-wrote the definition of idleness as a state of dejection that gave rise to torpor of mind, feeling and spirit. It devised a creeping sluggishness that leads to a poisoning and killing of the will, even though the Church's sole aim over centuries had been to poison and break the will of every peasant from Land's End to Constantinople. It painted idleness as despair, faintheartedness and a lack of desire for anything. The Church even extended idleness to include tolerance, which was especially handy when alien religions needed putting down.

From the year 1290 until the time that Cromwell defeated the King in the English Civil War 350 years later, it was illegal to be Jewish in England. Why? Because they weren't Christians? In theory, yes. In practice it was because they were not only non-Christians, but more importantly, generally successful merchants and the like. Moreover, as non-Christians they didn't pay their dues to the established Church. The Church didn't think much of this, so they invoked the Sin of Sloth. Up until the end of the thirteenth century, the general populace of England had been pretty tolerant of 'foreigners'. This

In 1290, someone born in London would have understood no more than a handful of words spoken by a person born in Norfolk.

was at a time when a 'foreigner' could mean someone who was born just a few miles away. In 1290, someone born in London would have understood no more than a handful of words spoken by a person born in Norfolk. Anyone who has taken a holiday on the Broads recently will understand how that could be the case.

It wasn't until the Church discovered that to be tolerant was to be idle and to be idle was to be slothful, that the Jews were rounded up and expelled, or in one extreme case, burned alive by the enthusiastic people of York. To avoid sinning through sloth, something had to be done. This legacy survived. During the Napoleonic wars, French vessels were frequently wrecked off the coast of England. Few French ever survived, however, as in those days sailors weren't allowed to learn to swim. If they did, they might abandon ship in the middle of an especially bloodthirsty battle and we couldn't have that, could we? Even in the First World War, pilots weren't given parachutes in case they jumped out of burning aircraft instead of trying to land them safely to be repaired and re-used.

This blind intolerance lives on, tragically, to our modern 'civilised' times and can be traced directly back to the Church's teachings about the dire consequences of the deadly Sin of Sloth.

SAINT OR SINNER?

German Professor Peter Axt actively recommends sloth for health and long life. The teutonic prof recently co-authored a study entitled *On the Joy of Laziness* in which he stated: 'People who would rather laze in a hammock instead of running a marathon or who take a midday nap instead of playing squash have a better chance of living into old age.' Which, of course, we always knew to be true.

Now that you are reaching the end of *Sin to Win*, it is time for me to make a confession. I have an unnatural distrust of religion. I'm not one for rules and regulations, I don't like being told what to do and I like to question everything.

To be fair, it is not only religious rules that I don't hold close to my heart, there are many laws of the land that I just don't understand. Why is it that Lord Archer of Super-Mare is allowed to graze his cattle on the common, while I can't? Why can't a boy under the age of ten see a naked mannequin? Why is it is legal for a male to urinate in public, as long it is on the rear wheel of his motor vehicle and his right hand is on the vehicle? Why is placing a postage stamp upside down on an envelope considered treason, punishable by death?

Why is placing a postage stamp upside down on an envelope considered treason, punishable by death?

Why is Sunday the only day of rest?

The first six Deadly Sins were easy for me to argue against. I take great exception to the Church telling me how much is enough, how I should feel about myself, and how to control my anger. Sloth, on the other hand, I find more challenging. We all associate success with hard work. Nothing, apparently, comes easily. We are all taught that we get out of life what we put in. These rules, I'm afraid, are true. With the exception of lottery winners, the Royal Family and Anne-Nicole Smith, we all need to work hard if it's money we covet. But working hard and employing the Sin of Sloth aren't mutually exclusive.

There is a theory called the eighty/twenty principle. It is said that twenty percent of a company's clients provide eighty percent of the profit. Twenty percent of a workforce delivers eighty percent of the sales. Twenty percent of a working day's effort produces eighty percent of its achievements. It makes sense that the rest of the day is being wasted. I remember when I first worked in a large office block that the workers' motto was 'Never look out of the window before lunch time'. This was because it left you with nothing to do in the afternoons! When a minor member of the Royal Family visited our office to open a new wing, the Duke of Sidcup, or whoever he was, asked, 'How many people work here?' The audible murmur amongst the assembled employees came back: 'About half of us.'

The avoidance of sloth and the negative effects of that avoidance still take many forms in business. If you are doing a mundane job that takes about three hours a day, but you are required to be at your desk for eight hours a day, you probably won't give your best even for the short time that you are actually working. This can lead to 'suit jacket syndrome', whereby enterprising young executives who want to get out during the day have a spare suit jacket at the office that they hang over the back of their chairs when they disappear for hours on end.

Not that I'm advising this as a route to success. Sloth, as with the six sins that precede it, has its time and place.

Some ask 'Why put off till tomorrow what can be done today?'

They obviously don't have enough work to do today.

Management brought up on the 'work' ethic of 'more time equals less sloth' are often blind to the truth of their own operation's inefficiency. When I shared another office in the same building, I found myself working alongside an accountant. His real job took no more than half the day, but he was always busy. He was constantly on the phone talking about corporation tax and whether VAT was reclaimable on materials supplied from other EC states, or poring over balance sheets. Knowing what I did about this organisation, at first I assumed that I had found the only person in the company who had a full-time job. And I had. He was an accountant. But not a company accountant – he was running his own private accountancy business from their office in their time and using their telephone and stationery. He had realised years previously that he had plenty of

THE SIN OF SLOTH – K-MART

If sloth is sitting back and sticking to what you know best then the history of K-Mart is a study in slothfulness. The firm has spent more than a hundred years turning a good buck out of the same trick – selling it cheap. The company is one of America's outstanding discounters, in a field that is not short of competition.

Sebastian Spering Kresge opened his first Kresge five-and-dime store at the end of the nineteenth century, and had expanded to 85 stores within 20 years, but it was the Great Depression that really validated the business philosophy. In 1962 the first K-Mart discount department store opened its doors in Michigan, and the number had swelled to 16 less than four years later, adding to the more than 750 Kresge stores.

At various points since then, whenever the firm is judged to have lost its way, it goes back to basics and re-emphasises its discounting credentials. 'Quality products at exceptional values', it says. And it works, with more than one hundred years of uninterrupted service to back that up.

time on his hands and had started the business with the intention of building it up to viability before giving up his day job. He did give up the day job, but in a long fit of sloth, just never quite got around to telling his employer.

Not only did he not have to pay for an office, he actually got paid merely for sitting in it.

There is a story about a boss who does in fact notice that one of his workers seems to have sunk into a fit of despairing sloth and obviously isn't giving his best. So, the boss invites the employee, let's call him David, into his office for a friendly, caring, interpersonal-relationships-type chat.

'What's wrong, David? I know you are a conscientious, hard worker, usually, but these last few weeks you seem a bit down. You're arriving late and your work seems to be suffering. Is there anything wrong here that I can help with?'

David is one of those who has got to the stage where he can do his job standing on his head, in about ten minutes a day, and is starting to find it difficult to conceal the fact. He may be showing all the symptoms of bored depression, and sinking into the trough of sloth, but he's hardly like to admit it to his boss. Instead, he blames his condition on his personal life. The job keeps him away from his wife a lot. When they are together, the kids are around and they don't have any quality private time together. The boss has the solution.

'David,' he says, 'I get like that sometimes with my wife. And do you know what I do? I go home early before the kids get home from school. I take her a bunch of flowers, a box of chocolates and good bottle of wine, and in return she gives me a nice, slow blowjob. The next day, I feel refreshed and keen for work again. Why don't you try that? Take the afternoon off and I'll see you tomorrow.'

David goes off for the rest of the day and returns the next morning. The boss invites him for a post-event chat. David tells him that he did exactly as he had been told: he took the gifts round and enjoyed a whale of a time. Then David says: 'Thanks very much, Boss. By the way, I like those red curtains you have in your bedroom.'

Even the hardest working over-achievers amongst us need to use a portion of sloth now and again. We need holidays to recharge our mental and physical batteries. I recently met someone who works extremely hard and makes a good living – simply because he is lazy. He is proud to be lazy. He detests work with a passion. In fact, he hates work vigorously. A few years ago he realised how much he hated his work and how much energy he was putting into hating his work, so he decided to re-channel this energy born of sloth to good effect. At the time he was a wage-slave employee, albeit a very well paid wage-slave with handsome benefits. But as is the case with most employees in other people's organisations, no matter how hard you work, there are limits to the extra benefits this will bring. He figured out that by applying the effort he was putting into hating working hard into simply working hard, he would only have to work half the time. He gave up his day job, and now works likes a slave for six months of the year and then has six months holiday. In the half-year that he works, it's so intensive he doesn't have time to hate it. In the half-year that he is off, he has so much fun, that he can face work again in the certain knowledge that he'll soon be relaxing by the Mediterranean again. For six sunny months.

I take her a bunch of flowers, a box of chocolates and good bottle of wine, and in return she gives me a nice, slow blowjob.

S A I N T   O R   S I N N E R ?

Churchill slept every afternoon, Hitchcock catnapped at parties and Napoleon slept on the battlefield. But Mexican General Antonio Lopez de Santa Ana takes the biscuit for wilful sloth in the face of danger. De Santa Ana always insisted on having a siesta, regardless of his military predicament. In 1836 he found himself surrounded by the Texan army but still had a kip in a wood. The Mexicans were routed in twenty minutes when the Texans attacked, but Santa Ana escaped!

We need short cuts to make the working day
more efficient, in effect, to fit more working
hours into the same time available.

**This bonus time, which is free, can be used
to make more money, or provide more leisure time or a
combination of both.**

You may think the story of our man who gave up his job to work hard half the time is all very well in a theory, but we can't all do that. He really does exist, and he modelled himself on another wage slave who stopped working full time and made himself a fortune, albeit not in quite the same way.

One of the cardinal rules of marketing is learned from the customer-product base grid. A business survives on two elements: products and customers. You don't need a degree from Harvard Business School to work out that these are the two essential assets any business needs to survive. Think of a business which is up and running – it has its existing products and its existing customers, but is facing competition or needs extra revenue for whatever reason and wants to expand its sales. Most businesses that never expand their sales fail. So what do most businesses do? They try to sell more of their products by finding more customers to sell them to. If they can't do that they try to sell more additional products to more customers.

Quite right too?

Wrong. They are not only doing things the hard way, they are doing it the wrong way. The most important asset above any other is the customer base, not the product base. How many times have you heard someone say 'I'm in the insurance business' or 'I'm in textiles' or 'We're in oil' or 'My company sells cars'? They are all looking at their businesses the hard way, the non-slothful way.

What all these companies are in, is the customer business. But they don't know it.

If they are selling their existing products to existing customers, most companies then try to sell existing products to new customers. When new customers don't buy their existing products, they try to sell new products to new customers. They diversify. Groovy, sexy, clever old them. They've ignored the slothful man's way of marketing efficiently and profitably. If you've got a customer, you have the best asset there is. You have done the hard work. Sit back and enjoy the benefits. Sell him something else. Sell him anything. He is the hardest thing to find. Any fool can make cars. Any idiot can churn out plastic extrusions. It doesn't take a rocket scientist to underwrite insurance.

If you've got a customer, you have the best asset there is. You have done the hard work. Sit back and enjoy the benefits. Sell him something else.

There is a lot of old rubbish churned out on the 'repeat it every season' television networks of today, but the Ronnie Barker comedy *Open All Hours* shouldn't be tarred with that brush. Roy Clarke, the series' writer, understands more about marketing than a whole year's worth of Harvard graduates. No matter what minor item someone goes into that shop to buy, they always come out with far more under their arm. If it's a box matches on the way in, a box of matches and 20 Rothmans on the way out. If it's a loaf of bread that's needed, a large sliced white, a small step ladder and some paint brushes are carried out. If it's someone merely asking directions, he sells them a map, a compass and pair of stout walking shoes.

THE SIN OF SLOTH – ASTRAZENECA

It isn't easy being a drug company these days. You have to spend a lot of money on research and development in the hope that you can come up with something good. No wonder there is so much consolidation in the industry as the big firms join forces to mitigate the expense. But – and it's a big but – when you get it right you get it very right. Develop something popular in the ulcer, cholesterol or antidepressant lines – the three biggest sectors for prescription drugs – and you could be doing very nicely.

Take AstraZeneca, formed out of the fusion in 1999 of the UK-based Zeneca Group and Sweden's Astra. It produces an ulcer treatment called Losec (or Philosec in the US), which is the world's best-selling prescription drug. It made the firm $6 billion in 2000, accounting for 40% of the firm's sales. If sitting back and creaming the profits from some intellectual property is corporate sloth then this is serious sloth.

And while the developed world's expensive taste for pharmaceuticals continues to expand unimpeded, it is no wonder that the drug companies are increasingly comfortable among the global corporate elite.

Watch it. It's free and you can sit in front of the telly with a beer while you learn, the slothful way.

'Six-months-a-year-man' learned this from a story that went round the organisation where he'd been employed. Someone in their sales force was under pressure to increase sales. He was told to get out and knock on a few doors, but he was, in classical terminology, lazy. Idle git he may have been, but he had worked hard on not having to work hard. One of his products was a specialist line of toothpaste. It was one of those supplied in faux Victorian packaging in an effort to make it appear traditional and wholesome. But the market was limited. Just about everyone who needed, or even wanted, Victorian toothpaste was already buying it.

Instead of wearing his knuckles down to the bone, knocking on the doors of reluctant shopkeepers who couldn't shift any more stock than they already had, he took a short trip to the factory that made their toothpaste tubes. Within weeks of that one short meeting, he increased his sales by over 30 percent. If he couldn't sell more product to new customers, he would get the existing ones to buy more of it. He got the tube manufacturer to increase the diameter of the cap nozzle by a small amount. He told them it was something to do with EC regulations and metrication, and they happily modified the item while grumbling about Brussels.

Few ever noticed that they were picking up a new tube of toothpaste every four weeks instead of every six. Who would?

That small change in diameter, which went unnoticed by the customers, increased the volume of paste squeezed with every mornings' brush by a third. They used more, they bought more. Few ever noticed that they were picking up a new tube of toothpaste every four weeks instead of every six. Who would?

SAINT OR SINNER?

Bertrand Russell, despite being perhaps the most noteworthy philosopher of the twentieth century and a highly industrious academic, was a great advocate of sloth. In 1932 he wrote an essay entitled 'In Praise of Idleness' in which he argued for a four hour working day. Perhaps even more excitingly, Russell saw such inactivity as an essential aspect of a complete social revolution that would take power away from those least suited to it. Hear, hear.

Your most expensive commodity is time.
Gluttony teaches us to cram more
life into the time we have.
Sloth teaches us to cram more
time into the life we have.

Success comes when you find your balance.

Jack Smethwick was a miner working in a grim pit village in the north of Yorkshire. He was basically a slothful type, but going down the pit was the only job available. He stuck it for a few years after leaving school, but soon became fed up with working two miles underground in the pitch black, waiting for the onset of lung disease, so he decided to emigrate to Australia, where he'd heard you could work in the mornings, get paid well, and enjoy the sunshine in the afternoons. He invited all his colliery mates to the pub one Friday night, they all got drunk and off he went the following morning to board a ship at Liverpool docks with his assisted-passage ticket. He sailed off to Sydney never, so his mates thought, to be seen again.

Twenty-five years later, and the pits are shut. Thatcher and Scargill have had their fight, and the former pit workers are sitting idly in the street wondering what they'd done to deserve the smelly end of life's stick in their faces, when a convertible pink Cadillac comes around the corner. It's driven by a sun-tanned man of perhaps 45 years of age, and sitting next to him is gorgeous blonde with a chest like a pair of ski jumps. One of the ex-miners recognises Mr Suntan. It's Jack.

His old mates gather round the car to ogle his trophy wife and then they all troop off to the Whippet and Wipe It pub for few jars to catch up on old times. Naturally, Jack's long-lost mates from his days as a miner are fascinated to hear how he came to be driving a flash car, dripping with gold and with a former super-model on his arm.

'Well,' he starts, 'I landed in Sydney and didn't know what to so, so I took the first bus I saw to the outback. I got off at the last stop and stood there, still with no idea of what I was going to do. I had about fifteen dollars left in my pocket, no job and nowhere to live. So I took a look at the few shops in this tiny town. In the window of one was a small ad that read "Shed for sale. $10". So I went round and saw the bloke and bought his shed. I fixed it up, gave it a lick of paint and sold it for $25. With that, I took a fiver out for food and lodgings and used the rest to buy two more second-hand sheds. I did them up, painted them, re-felted the roofs and sold them at a profit. With that profit, I bought four more sheds and refurbished them. After a few years' hard work, I was doing up about two thousand sheds a year and was the

A great deal of harm is being done in the modern world by belief in the virtuousness of work...

biggest second-hand shed supplier in New South Wales. Then my uncle died and left me ten million quid, so I thought, "Sod the sheds."'

As no less an authority than the philosopher Bertrand Russell wrote in his 'In Praise of Idleness':

I want to say, in all seriousness, that a great deal of harm is being done in the modern world by belief in the virtuousness of work, and that the road to happiness and prosperity lies in an organised diminution of work . . .

Modern technique has made it possible to diminish enormously the amount of labour required to secure the necessaries of life for everyone. This was made obvious during the war. At that time all the men in the armed forces, and all the men and women engaged in the production of munitions, all the men and women engaged in spying, war propaganda, or Government offices connected with the war, were withdrawn from productive occupations. In spite of this, the general level of well being among unskilled wage earners on the side of the Allies was higher than before or since.

Which is a long-winded way of telling the sheds story, but nonetheless holds even truer today.

We can all give ourselves the choice either to work less for the same reward, or work more for more reward.

There was a businessman who retired to the Essex coast. Like a lot of newly retired folk, he quickly became bored and wanted something to occupy the mind for a few hours a day. He took a look around the seaside town and finally decided to buy a small slot-machine games arcade. This was one of those places where the walls are covered with one-armed bandits. There was little involved in running this business, other than emptying the machines, doing a little paperwork and organising the maintenance and cleaning of the premises.

As the arcade was very busy in the season, and took a lot of holiday traffic, it needed regular and thorough cleaning. Most of these places are pretty filthy, but this man held a sort of pride in keeping a clean arcade. He couldn't actually afford to have the premises cleaned, as this would have taken more than his entire weekly profit, but he certainly didn't want to do the cleaning himself. Keeping occupied was one thing. Wielding a vacuum cleaner, mops and buckets first thing in the morning was something else.

He would arrive every Friday morning at 7.00 let the cleaners in for two hours, and at 9.00, just before he opened to the public, he paid the cleaners their weekly wages.

He paid them with the coins taken out of his machines. By no later than about a quarter to ten, the cleaners had put their entire wages back into his machines.

And there he had it – free cleaning services thanks to his own command of sloth.

There are many simple ways to save money and even make money by being lazy. Just recently I was buying fish at the local supermarket. The fish was fresh and looked good but was expensive. It was also unfilleted. As is often the way with modern supermarkets, their specialist counter staff are made up of local tradesmen who have been driven out of business by competition from these very supermarkets. Before my fish was weighed and paid for, I asked for it to be filleted. This is a service a trained fishmonger finds perfectly normal to perform for nothing and it was expertly done with a smile.

Even better than that, because the fish was lighter after being filleted, it was cheaper. Because I couldn't be bothered to fillet the fish for myself, I not only saved time and effort, but was also in effect given a discount against the ticket price. A superior service for a lower price: yet another example of laziness in action.

THE SIN OF SLOTH – COKE

Coke, as the biggest brand name in the world, doesn't seem an obvious candidate for sloth. But have a close look at what it does and you'll be surprised at how little it gets its fingers sticky for a firm of such magnitude. Basically, it makes syrup. And counts the money that pours in from every corner of the globe.

The bottling, the distribution and all the other risky stuff has been offloaded to subsidiaries, majority or minority-owned. Coke just operates a handful of plants churning out the concentrate that is sold on to the bottlers and then oversees the marketing.

That slothfulness put Coke well ahead of the pack as one of the first major corporations to practice such extreme outsourcing. It has tried a more energetic approach – diversifying into all sorts of areas over time, even the movie business in the 1980s. But it pulled back into its ultra-core, mindful that sometimes slothfulness pays off. Coke understands the 80/20 principle and practices it to a slothful T.

The Nine Commandments
of committing the sin of

SLOTH

---

1 Never do a job yourself that someone else will do for nothing.

Another character of Ronnie Barker's was Fletch, the recidivist inmate in *Porridge*. For few months before his release from a sentence for theft of a bundle of cash (which had never been recovered), he sent letters to his wife, which appeared to be coded messages. They all contained references to the garden. 'If you are feeling a bit down, my love, why not spend some time in the garden.' 'I am so looking forward to getting out and doing a bit of work in my beloved garden.' 'What fun we're going to have, enjoying our lovely garden again.'

The authorities of course read all letters from prisoners. The week before he was due to go home, a band of policemen turned up at his house with a warrant and a set of spades and systematically dug over the entire garden.

Unbeknown to the law, the cash was actually in a suitcase in the loft, but Fletch got his neglected garden dug over for nothing just in time for his release.

2 If it ain't broke, don't fix it.

Pepsi Cola spent the equivalent of the gross national product of a small country in changing the colour of their cans to blue. Not only did it not increase their sales, people actually bought less. They were too used to seeing cola in a red can, and it was a red can they automatically picked up.

Sales of Coke, in good old red cans, went up at the same time.

3 Doing nothing is often the best course of action.

Harley-Davidson is the oldest established manufacturer of motorcycles in the world. Most modern bikes drip with multi-cylinder engines, space-age technology frames and state-of-the-art sticky racing rubber. Not Harleys. America's best-selling bikes are virtually unchanged from the design they settled on back in the 1930s. They are the equivalent of a two wheeled tractor and handle like a knackered JCB on a frozen boating lake. But that's how the customers like them, so the company hasn't changed them.

Porsche's 911 is similar. Porsche settled on the 911 shape, with the air-cooled engine stuck out behind the rear wheels, forty years ago. When they introduced a water cooled 911, it bombed. When they tried to replace the 911 with the 928, with its front-mounted V8 engine, they sold a few, but then had to kill it off and reverted to the 911, complete with its ancient air-cooled engine sitting where the boot should be.

4 Even hard workers have a bit of sloth in them.

The number of days off ranks in the top three critical 'wants' of a soon-to-be employee when choosing their employer. Simply put, we all need to take time out to recharge, reflect and re-engage for the next task.

Microsoft understands this perfectly. They've employed enough receptionists, personal assistants and telesales executives to know how important time-out is to an individual. That's why they install 'Mine sweep' and 'Solitaire' on every office PC. The market research division cleverly deduced that by including a simple relaxation tool with their operating system, Microsoft products would win approval for the people that really mattered – their consumers.

5 Always go to work when you're ill.

For two good reasons.

One: if you have a rotten dose of the flu and you feel like death, why take a day off? What are going to do with your day, feeling like that? Be ill on someone else's time, not your own.

Two: if you do feel like having a day off, when you phone in sick your boss will think you really must be ill to actually take a day off, as he's knows how terrible you looked the last time you struggled in.

6 Read *Viz*.

Viz magazine has a page of handy tips for lazy people. For example, if you can't be bothered to wash and iron your shirts, but don't want to waste money on expensive laundry bills, give all your dirty shirts to Oxfam every Friday. The nice charity ladies will wash and iron them and you can buy them all back on Monday.

In fact, this act of sloth was stolen by a large international chain of burger bars for an advertising campaign. Their agency, like most advertising agencies, doesn't waste time thinking up good original ideas when there are hundreds of them just waiting to be picked up for nothing.

7 Find an easier way to do things.

Another top tip from *Viz* magazine concerns a burning issue for the nation's tomato growers. By digging a trench four feet deep alongside your plants, you'll be able to step inside and find the tomatoes are conveniently at chest height – thus eliminating backache.

This may sound like a silly gag, but serves a practical purpose for those wanting to commit the Sin of Sloth. Through creative thinking, we can all find easier ways of doing things. Often, the easier way will save time and money – or both.

8 Don't care.

Sloth is often interpreted as a sense of not caring. But not caring about what? Those who have made themselves truly successful often share the ability to not care about failure. There is an old adage that anyone who has never failed in business hasn't been trying hard enough. But, in truth, those who don't fail don't care about failing. It was scientists who, through caring about the natural history of aerodynamics, proved that bees can't fly.

Bees don't give a monkey's – they do it anyway.

9 The slothful way is usually the most efficient way.

The only effort that is never wasted is the effort you put into finding ways to avoid wasted effort.

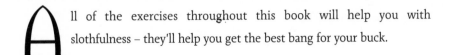

Exercise on

SLOTH

All of the exercises throughout this book will help you with slothfulness – they'll help you get the best bang for your buck.

◆ Make sure you are 'playing from a ten'. Use the anchoring exercise described in 'Pride' to conjure up a positive state from thin air. If you are in the most resourceful state of mind, the right actions to move you towards your goals will follow easily and effortlessly.

◆ Don't slave away scrabbling towards achievement through trial and error. Get envious and then steal someone else's recipes for success – and benefit from all of their hard work.

◆ Use your imagination to accelerate your progress. You can mentally rehearse something while sitting in a comfy chair with a nice cup of cocoa.

◆ Get some clear goals so you focus your efforts on what you really want.

◆ Get angry -flick the pain/pleasure switch and take some action, instead of grumbling and doing nothing.

. . . well those are a few examples, but in the spirit of slothfulness I'm not going to do the hard work for you, go figure the rest out for yourself.

One last model to leave you with, it's one we call the 'DANCE' model. Do you remember we talked about that fly, smacking itself against the windowpane time and time again, trying to get out? The phrase 'work smarter, not harder' – the motto of slothfulness – was invented to avoid the shenanigans of our six-legged friend. Work smarter is what the DANCE model is all about. It works as follows:

D   Have a desired outcome – have **a** goal.

A   Take action – do something to work towards that goal.

N   Notice the results you get from your actions.

C   Change your approach – be flexible – if you are not getting the
        results you want.

E   Aim for excellence. Make your efforts as slick as possible – keep refining so
        you reach your goals more effectively and efficiently.

Take a moment and make a list of things that are taking up a lot of your time and effort at the moment. Things that keep popping up and sapping your energy. A classic example is the 'to-do grenade' at work. You know the type of thing I mean – you have a whole list of things on your list for a day and this one thing, the to-do grenade, shatters your plans as soon as it falls into your lap.

Pick one thing off your list and work through the DANCE model:

D   What is your desired outcome?

A   What have you been doing to date? What actions have you tried?

N   What results have you achieved?

C   What other approaches might work?

E   What would be a really slick approach to try?

Take the spirit of slothfulness to heart as you go through steps C and D.

◆ What would be the most resourceful state of mind to be in as you tackle this?

◆ What approaches might someone you are really envious of take?

◆ What would be the most slothful thing to do?

Did you come up with some different ideas to try? Great. Take pride in the results of your slothfulness and channel your energy into more sinning for winning.

REVELATIONS

'We may become the makers of our fate when
we have ceased to pose as its prophets.'

Karl Popper – Philosopher

'People like me were branded, pigeon-holed, a ceiling put on our ambitions.'

John Prescott – Deputy PM & Heavyweight Boxer

ONE ESTATE AGENT IN LONDON HAS A SPECIAL RELATIONSHIP with Christianity. On a good week, he might go to church a dozen times. No two churches are the same to him. He breathes in the stained-glass windows. He eyes up the tall steeple. He inspects the ornate brickwork. He breathes in the tranquility of the peaceful surrounding gardens. And along with the fragrance of the now overrun hydrangeas and wisteria, he smells an opportunity. At the turn of the twentieth-century, 56% of British children attended Sunday School. At the turn of the twenty-first, that figure stands at less than 4%. With attendance at churches in freefall, and vicars nailing boards over their stained glass windows, this estate agent has a lot of empty buildings to sell.

Christianity, one of the very first global businesses, relies on one emotion to help sell its message. Fear. And for the last fifty years or so, we Brits have had very little

Like the cuts of meat that are now prettily displayed in supermarkets rather than as the corpses of dead animals hanging in butchers' shop windows, war still happens, but in a sanitised, distant way.

to be afraid of. Apart from a handbags-at-dawn scrap with Argentina, a couple of scuffles with Saddam, and a quick foray into Korea to help the United States stop the creep of Communism, we haven't been properly at war since 1945. That was the last time war affected those of us at home who had no direct personal contact with the armed forces. Any conflict that has occurred has been hermetically shrink-wrapped for us, isolated from our island home and displayed for us on television screens if we want to watch. Like the cuts of meat that are now prettily displayed in supermarkets rather than as the corpses of dead animals hanging in butchers' shop windows, war still happens, but in a sanitised, distant way.

Our quality of life is greater now than it has ever been. Few of us now ever have to pick up a rifle and go to war. Few of us ever get bombed out during the night. Few of us will ever get to parachute behind enemy lines. And quite apart from the population-sapping ravages of life-threatening, international armed conflicts, our general state of health has improved. Life expectancy at birth has doubled in the last 150 years. No longer do women have to give birth to half-a-dozen or more offspring in the hope that one or two will survive to adulthood. And because we're living longer, and fully expect to live longer from the moment of our first conscious thought, we're now not so afraid of dying.

Without fear, why would we pray?

On 11 September 2001, two planes crashed into the twin World Trade Center Towers in New York. A third plane destroyed a section of the Pentagon in Washington. At least two others failed to meet their intended targets. No one will ever know the reason why such an atrocity happened; all we know is that the suicide-hijackers took control of the flights (and up to 6,000 innocent lives) in the name of their religion. It seems they interpreted Islam in a different way to the millions of peaceful, loving, caring Muslims around the world.

The Western world was shocked, then outraged. And quite rightly so.

And then the strangest thing happened, we worried ourselves crazy that London or any other of our major cities could be the next target. We realised just how fragile life is. We panicked every time a plane roared over our heads. We feared traveling. We wanted to be rescued. We wanted to be told that we were on the side of good, not evil. We became afraid, and so we started to pray.

Church attendance shot up to levels not seen since the Second World War.

Of course, the Church's renaissance will be short lived. In time, we will forget how scared we were. As the pictures of missiles hurtling into Afghanistan were relayed around the Western world, once again we became reassured and we started, almost unconsciously, to push religion to the backs of our minds and started to get on with our daily routines.

The estate agent will soon go back to selling derelict churches to property developers.

Meanwhile, as those missiles screamed overhead across the north-west Himalayan Mountains, thousands of Afghan refugees returned from the countryside to the very cities that were being destroyed by sophisticated American hardware.

Why? Because en masse they wanted to go to a mosque.

We have different cathedrals in which to worship regularly on a Sunday now. For many of us, it's the out-of-town hypermarket...

Most of us lead perfectly good lives more or less in accordance with the teachings of whichever Church we were born into, whether it be Christian, Jewish, Muslim, Buddhist, Sikh or any other. Most of us live more or less to the fundamental codes of conduct we learned as children. Most of us in Britain do in fact follow these rules instinctively. Very few of us ever commit murder or GBH or rob banks or bash little old ladies over the head for their pension books. We know these things are wrong and the thought of doing them never enters our heads. But even though we follow the teachings of the Church, most of us don't feel the need to go to a church.

Of course, many of us get married in a church, but in truth this is more likely because it's a pretty building, the music is nice, and the seating is perfectly arranged, with an aisle neatly dividing the seating into two separate sections for the rival family tribes to eye each other, before they get a chance to have go at the finger buffet in celebration of their newly found status as in-laws. And many of us will have our funerals in a church; although for obvious reasons we don't often get much say in how or where that particular ceremony is conducted.

We have different cathedrals in which to worship regularly on a Sunday now. For many of us, it's the out-of-town hypermarket, where the weekly shop has taken the place of the weekly prayer. For others, it might be the huge DIY store, where we worship at the altar of home improvement, having been converted to the cause by the disciples of the Lord of the Rag Roll Technique on countless television shows. For many, it might just be an evangelistic zeal for the Great God Leisure. And yet, just a few years ago, nothing was open on a Sunday in Britain. A trip to the West End of London on a Sunday afternoon was akin to visiting a ghost town that had been deserted even by the ghosts. Today, on a Sunday, the city streets are more crowded than just about any other day. Everything is open. Shops, bars, cafes, museums and art galleries all have their doors wide open and their tills are overflowing. In fact, the only buildings you will find shut on a Sunday are the churches. Unless, of course the agent has a prospective buyer who might be keen to convert.

All this leisure activity is yet another sign that we live in an age where we no longer fear everyday life. Where we no longer have that need to pray for forgiveness and salvation. In age where we no longer die in our thousands of the plague, nor live in constant fear of being overrun by hoards of pillaging Goths, Huns or Vikings, nor shelter in our Underground stations while smartly dressed young men drop high explosives from 25,000 feet on to our houses, we have other ways to occupy our Sundays.

But are we not in fact still replicating that trip to church? Do we continue to have that in-bred need for the shared experience, that requirement to be packed into a public building along with a lot of like–minded souls to go through a ritual of shared experience? Go along to Ikea on a Sunday and you will jostle with hundreds of others in close proximity. To get there you will have queued on the M25 for an age and then waited patiently for a parking space. You'll queue to get in, and when you've found the items you want, you'll jostle again in line to take communion with the check-out girl.

Is what we're doing really any different to those who, 300 years ago, would have walked to Canterbury or York or Lincoln to join the queuing throngs in a great minster of those who felt the need to touch the ossified bones of an ancient saint from a distant land? Not at all. The process is the very same one. We may think our motives for making the trip are different. But are they? It's a ritual that by any logical measure none of us actually needs to make. But we go to B&Q, buy that patio heater or new towel rail or electric drill and we feel better, in exactly the same way as those ancient religious pilgrims who walked a thousand dusty miles before finally they staggered into the gloom of Santiago de Compastella to have a few drops of water splashed on them. They didn't know why they did it either. They had been told to do it. They believed they had to do it and so they did it. And they felt better.

We watch cable television and we know we have to make the visit. We've been told to do it. We do it and we feel better.

But if no-one had told we were missing something in our lives, would we ever have noticed? How many of us could survive without a television set in the house? Okay, we are all a bit sophisticated now, and at that dinner party when the subject comes up we all say, 'Actually I don't watch much television. It wouldn't bother me in the least if it went back to the shop to-morrow?' Really? Try it. Most of us wouldn't know what to do with ourselves. And yet, human beings have been on the go for the best part of 400,000 years. Television has managed about 40 years in the watchable form we know today. That's 0.01% of the time we've been on this planet that we have had television to watch, and yet most of us in the developed world would be at a loss to fill a few hours every single day without it.

So, for 99.99% of the time that we have existed on this planet, the television set wasn't here for us and yet if it breaks down, we feel as bereaved as if a close and much-loved family member has passed away unexpectedly right in front of our eyes. Of course it's not just the television. There's the car and the telephone and the mobile telephone and the computer and the laptop computer and the second car and countless other technological treasures to be heaped on the altar of our existence, and without which we feel as if something is missing. Without them we feel our lives are not complete.

And that is religion: fear. Not just a perfectly understandable fear of terrible things like the Black Death or a Norman invasion or the Blitz, but a nagging fear that we're missing out on something. Not anything in particular, not some tangible thing we could list on our portable electronic notepads, but just 'something'.

And with our continued form of religion – the consumerist evangelism that evolved quite naturally in accordance with the best rules of Darwinian theory – that is, our pursuit of happiness, peace and contentment through the shared experience of the superstore or the television show or the website or the text message, we need the baggage that goes with it.

Just as all those religions that existed long before the microchip or even the oven chip, there always has to be something else we need to think we require to be complete.

And what we need is sin. In fact, to really become complete, we need seven of them. Pride gives us a sense of self-belief, envy gives us something to strive for, gluttony takes the ceiling of our desires, lust rewards us for achieving short-term goals, anger gives us the passion to get things right, avarice keeps things on track. And sloth? Without sloth, is all the effort really worth it?

There: I've given you something to strive for that you didn't know you were missing until it was pointed out.

Nothing changes, does it?